Guide to Winning Elections

C. Douglas Conlan

ISBN-10: 1481141392
ISBN-13: 978-1481141390

DEDICATION

This book is dedicated to my mother Irene who taught me how to care for others. To my father John who taught me to strategize and think for myself. To my brother Kevin who taught me how to fight and be original. Most importantly, to my son Jack, who taught me how to be better.

.

CONTENTS

PROLOGUE

One of the penalties for refusing to participate in politics is that you end up being governed by your inferiors.—Plato

The purpose of this book is to dispel the common misconception that "my vote doesn't count." Your vote does count, and even more importantly your opinion and voice count.

Hopefully this project will get you started toward participating in the World's Greatest Political Debate EVER—the USA!

We stay a great country by the sheer will of our ability to constantly influence our government officials. Money certainly plays a part, but nothing is more powerful than an educated and participatory citizen. And nothing holds our elected officials more accountable than our actions as participants!

A January 2013 Rasmussen Poll showed that 53% of likely voters don't believe that **EITHER** Party represents the American people. 63% of Republicans believe their Party has "lost touch," yet more than **50% of Precinct Committeemen seats are UNFILLED**. The Democrats fare a little better in the wake of winning a close 2012 election, but still have an alarming number of unfilled Precinct Committeemen seats. **The Precinct is where the real power exists to change how our Representatives perform.**

It's not really a conspiracy that the powers that be have not afforded **THE PEOPLE**—the taxpayer, the student, the worker, the housewife, the minister, or the citizen—the proper education or tools with which to enable ourselves protection of our personal freedoms and reasonable, accountable government services.

The government has power because we give it to them by our action or inaction. We're busy living our lives, providing for our children, creating new technologies, serving in the military, paying taxes, and being Americans. We need to make time to participate.

Fortunately, our Founding Fathers put in place mechanisms for us to challenge authority, create policies that work for our own communities, and even change the overall structure of government if we so choose.

This book is not a Bible or even a handbook that might provide instantaneous solutions to the ongoing problems we face in our Republic. It is however a guideline, and hopefully, a thought provoking manuscript which enables all of us to join together, work together and "how to" move forward regardless of political party.

30 years ago there was a very specific ideological combat situation between Capitalism and Communism. Capitalism won. Now there is a very specific non-ideological combat situation between capitalism and community, and ideologically on specific issues. NOW we need to be Americans and join together to solve the problems that our government currently doesn't seem to be able to solve by itself.

You have power as an individual who is part of the process to make changes.

Demanding good government is not just about coming out of the closet, out of the woodshed, joining a union or issue group, rallying in the streets, churches, synagogues, or town halls. It's about rolling up our sleeves and getting our hands dirty from the local level all the way to the top.

Our Republic demands that we participate. Our citizenship is only as valuable as we make it. If we choose to ignore it, then we choose to give it no value, and ultimately lose our liberties.

Participate or be enslaved. Here are the basic tools for you.

"We are a people capable of self-government, and worthy of it."
—Thomas Jefferson to Isaac Weaver, Jr., 1807

HOW TO USE THIS BOOK

1. Chapters 1–10 are more of a basic book approach to how the political process works. Having a clear understanding of the evolution of the process will help provide a basis for creating and implementing an action plan according to Chapters 11-20.

2. Chapters 11–19 relate to using technology to maximize the effectiveness of your actions, whether you are acting as an individual citizen, a candidate or part of a team.

3. Chapter 20 shows you how you can influence legislation as an individual or form a group to become even more powerful to get the legislation passed that you want or stop legislation that you don't want.

4. Visit http://www.guidetowinningelections.com and register for free for up to date strategies and news about the changes in the landscape of political activism and elections.

1 INVOLVEMENT = POWER AND INFLUENCE

We have just come through one of the dirtiest election campaign in history. Candidates on every level accused each other of everything from being a socialist to being ultra conservative as if those were horrible things. Indiscretions from the time of birth were dragged out and aired on TV and YouTube, tweeted about and "Facebooked" together with anything derogatory in a candidate's background that could be dredged up or made up. By the time the candidates finished hanging out all the dirty laundry—whether real or created—and defaming each other's character, the voting public was left with this question: "Why would we want any of them to represent us anywhere?" The constituencies have lost confidence in their representative's ability to be honest and straightforward in doing the job. In essence, the public has been robbed of having confidence in their elected officials before they even get into office.

Politicians rate low on the polls related to professions in terms of honesty and integrity. For example, in a list of 40 professions listed by academy.com politicians ranked 39th just above the least favorite—telemarketers. In a 2010 Gallop poll rating honesty and ethical standards of politicians 57% rated them "very low," 32 % rated them "average" and only 9% rated them "high." Finally, a Rasmussion 2009 poll states "Often you hear people hating company CEOs, attorneys, or even Wall Street workers. But according to the newest Rasmussen poll, none of these professions compare to a member of Congress in terms of being least respected in America. 72% of those polled rated Congress as unfavorable, while 25% polled rated the job as favorable." But it's not just this past election that has disturbed us.

We continue witnessing corruption in the halls of government. If you Google "political scandals" you will receive thousands of pages of responses with lists of scandals attributed to every administration and all branches of government all the way back to George Washington. (Our search for "scandals in the United States government" revealed over 120,000,000 results. Yes, that *is* 120 million!).

Wikipedia makes this disclaimer about the subject: "To keep the article a manageable size, Senators and Congressmen who are rebuked, admonished, condemned, suspended, found in contempt, found to have acted improperly, used poor judgment or were reprimanded by Congress are *not* included unless the scandal is exceptional or leads to expulsion."

Excuse me! Just how long would the list be if they all *were* listed?

Sex scandals have peppered the news in every administration and even in Presidential campaigns. Of note were the President Bill Clinton escapades which resulted in impeachment for perjury. The impeachment was acquitted by the Senate (Isn't that another scandal?).

The John Edwards scandal surfaced during the 2008 Presidential campaign and he subsequently withdrew and was indicted on six counts, including conspiracy, four counts of illegal campaign contributions and one count of false statements. Not just a "little indiscretion." On May 31, 2012, Edwards was found not guilty on one count, and the judge declared a mistrial on the remaining five charges, as the jury was unable to come to an agreement. On June 13, 2012, the Justice Department announced that it dropped the charges and will not attempt to retry Edwards.

Then we have the Jack Abramoff scandal—a lobbyist found guilty of conspiracy, tax evasion and corruption of public officials in three different courts in a wide ranging investigation. Implicated in this scandal was Tom DeLay, the House Majority Leader who was reprimanded twice by the House Ethics Committee and convicted of two counts of money laundering and conspiracy in 2010. He was convicted in January 2011 and sentenced to three years in prison but was free on bail while appealing his conviction. In October of 2012 his attorney asked the judge to overturn the conviction. As of this writing there is no word on when the court will issue its ruling.

Scandals in government at all levels could fill several volumes but we have more trouble than just scandals.

Taxes have raced higher and higher. Inflation is eating us up, joblessness is at an all time high. Gas prices are soaring out of control. Homes continue to go to short sale and foreclosure and the number of homeless people continues to grow. Bankruptcies are a common occurrence and the banks are reticent to grant loans, while accepting billions in tax payer dollars. The picture does, at times, seem bleak indeed.

People are rightfully upset. The phrase from the movie "Network" is being used more frequently. Remember it? It is:

I'm as mad as hell and I'm not going to take it anymore.

There are basically three alternatives facing us when we look at this picture:

- One is to dismiss the problems as a symptom of "middle age depression" or some other malady and ignore it, hoping the problems will go away. Simply convince yourself, "America has *always* been a good country and it *always* will be no matter what."

- The second alternative is to throw up our collective hands and say, "There's no use! There's nothing I can do to make a difference anyway."

- And the third alternative is to *get involved and get people who hold similar values and political views as you involved along with you.*

"But," you say, "I only have one vote and that doesn't count for much." Wrong! Let's look at some past campaign results.

In the twenty first century things have improved somewhat in terms of voter turnout than we saw in the last election of the twentieth century.

1996	Clinton Vs. Dole	49% Voter Turnout
2000	Gore vs. Bush	50.4% Voter Turnout
2004	Bush vs. Gore	56.2% Voter Turnout
2008	Obama vs. McCain	61.6% Voter Turnout
2012	Obama vs. Romney	57.5% Voter Turnout (est)

3

In 2008 61.6% turned out to elect Barack Obama Obama was elected with 53.3% of that voting population. He was elected by 30.8% of the total number of eligible voters. (He received 69,498,516 of a possible 225,499,000 eligible voters). While the number of people voting has increased, 30.8% of the population is no mandate.

In 2010, a non-Presidential election year, only 37% of eligible voters bothered to go to the polls or mail in their ballot.

The numbers for the 2012 election are not final, but the existing numbers will give us a clear picture of what happened in the election which won't change with the final tally. According to the United States Elections Project (www.electionsgmu.edu) there were 240,926,957 people of voting age in the 2012 election. Of these 180,345,625 (76.8%) were registered to vote. Of these 62,611,250 voted to return Obama to the Presidency. So only 26% of those of voting age voted to return Obama to the Presidency and only 34.7% of registered voters voted for him. Hardly a mandate. He won the election by 51.42 % of votes cast. Hardly a mandate. It's interesting to note that in 2012 he received 6,881,126 fewer votes than he received in 2008, some of which can be attributed to a lower voter turnout.

CONGRESSIONAL RACES IN 2008 and 2012

The table below shows the voter turnout in the last five federal elections. Notice the drop in number of voters who voted in the Congressional elections even though they were already voting for the Presidential candidate—not much effort was needed to check a few more names lower on the ballot. There is even more drop off in those years in between Presidential elections. Not even a simple majority elected those Congressmen and Congresswomen who make the laws you have to obey.

Year	Population of voting age	% of voting-age population that voted for President	% of voting-age population that voted for US Representative
2012	240,926,957	57.5%	Data not available
2010	234,564,000	No Presidential campaign	37.0
2008	229,945,000	63.0%	53.3
2006	224,583,000	No Presidential campaign	35.7

Source: http://www.census.gov/compendia/statab/2012/tables/12s0398.pdf

The United States Congress is a powerful body, responsible for legislation that affects every facet of your life in America—laws that protect or jeopardize your freedom. Our future as a country depends to a great extent on the men and women elected to serve as our representatives in that important office. And yet only 37% bothered to vote in 2010—a non-Presidential election year.

STATE ELECTIONS

The further away you get from the Office of President, the fewer number of people bother to vote, especially in an election not held in conjunction with a Presidential election. Take Arizona, for example In the 2008 election:

Estimated voting age population	3,625,000
Registered voters	2,987,451
Percent of eligible voters registered	82.4%
Number voting for President	2,293,475
Number voting for Congressional seats	2,155,694
Total turnout percent	77.69%

In this election every Arizona who voted for a Presidential candidate also voted for a U.S. Representative (There was no Senate seat up for re-election).

However, only 1,698,135 people voted in 2010 —a 55.7% turnout. That's 22% less than voted for their U.S. Representatives in 2008. Where were the other voters? Taking a nap? Getting a mani-pedi?

PRECINCT POLITICS

Generally when we study voter turnout figures, we see that an average of about 60% of the registered voters turn out. Using this average, let us look at a precinct. An average precinct has several thousand people in it but for the purpose of clarification let us pretend that our precinct has 100 voters. The figures will look like this:

Voter age population	100
Registered to vote	70
Not registered to vote	30
Those voting	42
Those not voting	58

Now, applying these figures to a precinct with half Republican and half Democrat registration we see the following picture:

	Dem	Rep	Total
Voting age population	50	50	100
Persons registered	35	35	70
Persons NOT registered	15	15	15
Persons voting	21	21	21
Those NOT voting	29	29	29
Votes to win primary election	11	11	--

Why only eleven votes to win the primary election? It is very simple. You only need 50% plus one of those who do come out and vote. If 21 people go vote in the Democrat or Republican primary election, you only need eleven votes to win. Isn't that disgraceful? Only eleven people out of 100 can decide who is going to be the party's candidate in the general election. What does this mean to you? Quite simply it means that since few people take advantage of the right to exercise their franchise as voters, there are great political opportunities for the person who is willing to do some volunteer work as a neighborhood persuader! An election is won precinct by precinct, just as a building is built brick by brick.

PRECINCT BY PRECINCT?

➤ "But," you may contend, "I am only one person. What difference can I make?" Just in case you do not believe that elections are won precinct by precinct and vote by vote, let's take a look at some past election results showing you just how important one precinct and one vote is:

➤ In Minnesota's 2010 gubernatorial election Mark Dayton won with 43.7% of the vote. He had 8,770 votes more than his opponent Tom Emmer—winning by *just over 2 votes per precinct.* A recount was called for and, following the recount, Dayton was declared the winner.

➤ In 2008 Al Franken and Norm Coleman were the top two vote getters for the U.S. Senate in Minnesota. The Minnesota State Canvassing Board ordered a hand recount because the margin of victory was within one half of one percent. The recount took from November 8th until July 7th 2009 when Al Franken was sworn in. When the count was over he had won by 312 votes which is only 3/4 of one vote per precinct.

➤ In 1984 Indiana's Secretary of State certified Rick McIntyre as the winner by 34 votes, ignoring other recounted tallies that actually showed Frank McCloskey won by 0.00171 % We won't even try to figure out what the precinct vote margin was.

➤ In the 2004 gubernatorial race in Washington, Democrat Christine

Gregoire defeated Republican Dino Rossi following two recounts, after the initial count and first recount showed Rossi as the winner. Gregoire won by 133 voters in 6,719 precincts. This is 1/66th of a vote per precinct.

➢ In 2008 George Bush was declared the winner in Florida after a recount that gave him a margin of 537 votes. He won, then by 1/13th of a vote per precinct.

➢ In 1948 in Texas, Lyndon B. Johnson was elected to the U.S. Senate by 87 votes out of 988,295 votes cast in 6,000 precincts. That figures out to be 1/69th of a vote per precinct.

➢ In 1958 we re-elected six Congressmen to the U.S. House of Representatives by less than one vote per precinct.

➢ 1n 1960 John F. Kennedy defeated Richard M. Nixon by 113,000 votes nationwide — about one half vote per precinct.

➢ In 1970 in Kentucky, Roman Mazzoli was elected to the U.S. House of Representatives by two-thirds of a vote per precinct.

➢ In 1974 in a special election, John Murtha defeated Harry Fox by a total of 122 votes. There were 430 precincts in the district, making Murtha the winner by a margin of one-forth vote per precinct.

➢ In 1974 in Ohio James Rhodes defeated incumbent John Gilligan and was elected Governor by a margin of about 10,000 votes, less than one vote in each of Ohio's 12,800 precincts.

➢ In 1974 the outcome of U.S. Senate seats in New Hampshire and North Dakota were so close that both parties made challenges and counter challenges. Each demanded recounts. It was months before the issue was settled and the winners were finally certified. There was a ten vote margin in New Hampshire and a sixteen vote margin in North Dakota.

➢ In 1980 Senator Barry Goldwater (Presidential candidate in 1964, with three terms in the U.S. Senate) won re-election in Arizona by only 49.4% of the vote—8 votes per precinct.

➢ In 1980 John East of North Carolina won the U.S. Senate seat by one vote per precinct.

➢ In 1980 Jack Fields challenged a seven-term Congressman from the 8th District in Texas. At the outset of the campaign it was thought that unseating this fourteen year veteran would be impossible. However, the Fields team organized each precinct and did their homework so well they won by a vote margin of 4,935—41 votes per precinct.

➢ In 1980 in Pennsylvania, Marc Marks, the incumbent Congressman, defeated his opponent by only 120 votes—about one-third vote per precinct.

Let the figures speak for themselves. It is in the precinct that votes are gained and the election is won or lost. It is the precinct that has power and influence in politics. In the following chapters YOU can learn how to have this power and this influence.

Get it? YOU are not only important. Your vote is critical.

Now let's find out how you go about making a difference.

2 THE STRUCTURE OF POLITICS

The same tradition of free and constructive competition employed in America since the beginning, to provide the greatest good for the greatest number of people, has also given us our political system. Free competition between individuals to create, produce and sell goods and services that other individuals want to buy also applies to the political arena, just as it does to the economic field.

Basically, politics is simply the marketing of ideas regarding the operation of our government, and the selling of candidates who will implement those ideas. Rather than selling goods or services, a political party "markets" philosophy, platforms, programs, policies and candidates who best represent these ideas about government.

To understand just how and where you get involved in the setting of policies and electing candidates, it is essential to understand how a political party is structured and just where you can fit in. It really is very simple.

Just as government is structured at various levels—Federal, State and Local, so are the political parties structured. There is a *National committee, a State committee and local committees.* Let's take a closer look at each level.

NATIONAL COMMITTEE

The national committee of each party is comprised of three members from each state—a National Committeeman, a national committeewoman and the state party chairman. These are usually selected by the party at state levels by vote of the membership of the state committee.

The duties of the National Committee are large in scope. It is responsible for the operation of the party's national convention which selects the Presidential and Vice Presidential candidates. It generally establishes the party policies. It may call other conventions and meetings to conduct the party's national business as necessary.

The national committee also elects the party's national officers. It is traditional, however, for the national committee to accept the chairman and co-chairman of the party who has been recommended by that party's Presidential candidate. The National Chairman serves as the party spokesman. This is particularly important if his party is not in power, so that the "loyal opposition" has its views expressed.

Finally, the national committee works together with the party's Presidential campaign committee to conduct nationwide campaigns. It conducts major fund-raising efforts and it oversees the operations of the party's national funds, headquarters and staff.

STATE COMMITTEE

Our Constitution does not mention or make provisions for political parties. That was left up to the people and to the states; therefore, the structure and operation of political parties may vary widely from state to state.

What is presented here is a general review of typical party structure and operation at the state level. More complete details on how the parties are structured in your state can be found on the Internet. Google or search for Arizona or Texas or Michigan e.g., Republican Party, Democrat Party or Libertarian Party. If you cannot find the information you are searching for contact us at http://www.guidetowinningelections.com.

Now, down to business regarding the state committee.

The highest level of official party structure in each state is the State (central) Committee. See the charts following.

Typical Organization of a Political Party

NATIONAL COMMITTEE
Plans national convention to select candidates for Presidency and Vice-Presidency. Adopts party platform. Raises funds for candidates in their party.

STATE COMMITTEE
Selects delegates to national convention; works for election of party candidates to national and state offices; plans and directs party campaigns statewide.

COUNTY COMMITTEE
Made up of precinct committeemen from all precincts in the county. County committee officers are elected from all precinct committeemen. Works with precinct leaders; provides speakers, registration, publicity, finances, and education.

PRECINCT COMMITTEE
Each precinct has a precinct leader or chairman and precinct workers. They contact all new people in the neighborhood regarding political affiliations; see that members of their party get registered to vote; do other political canvassing; carry out election day activities to get only the "friendly voters" to the polls. This is where the power is—where elections are lost or won.

Typical State Party Structure

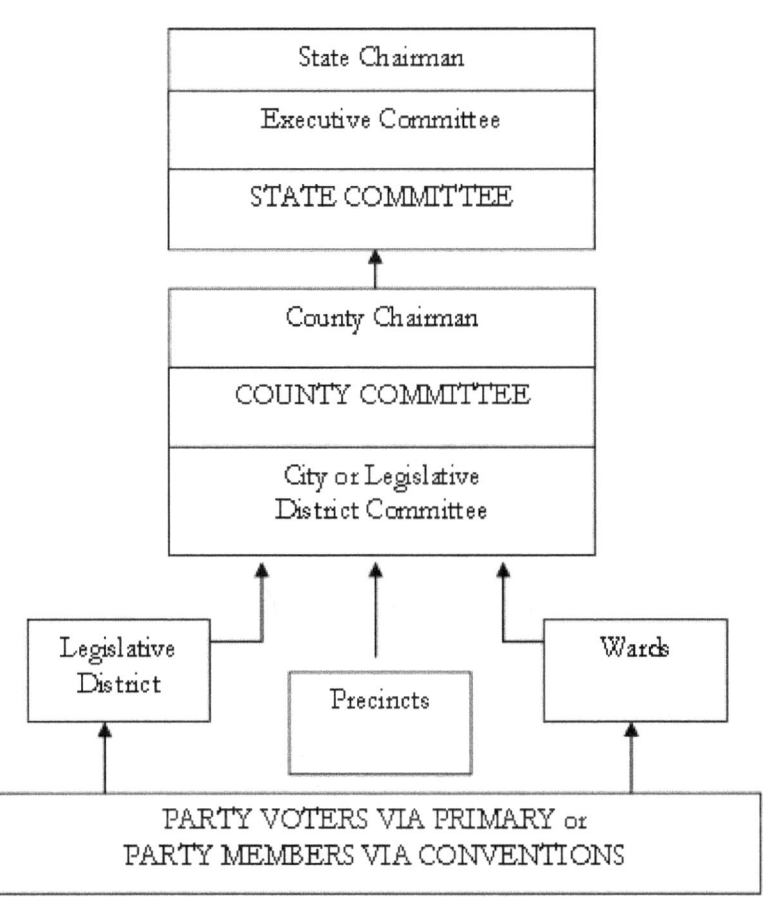

Because the make-up of the state committee varies so greatly from state to state, it is not possible to be specific about the composition of the committee. Therefore, the following list shows the kinds of representatives who may be included in a state committee:

- All or some of the chairmen of the party's county committees

- Delegates elected at the local level in precinct or district conventions

- The party's nominees for all partisan public offices

- The state chairman (or presidents) of the party's major volunteer groups

The state committee conducts the party's business at the state level. This includes direction of statewide campaigns in support of the party's candidates, the operation of the party's state headquarters and the hiring and the supervision of a professional staff, fund-raising efforts to finance the statewide campaigns, and financing the party's housekeeping operations. It is also responsible for convening the official party meetings as required by state law and such other meetings considered necessary to the committee's leadership.

In some states the state committee drafts and adopts the party platform; however, in other states a special state convention composed of the party's nominees for all partisan public offices drafts and approves the platform.

Generally, the state committee does not endorse candidates in a contested primary election, but functions only in the general election on behalf of the nominees selected in the party primaries.

COUNTY COMMITTEES

The major duty of the county committee is to elect its candidates to office and to gain a majority of the votes in the county for the party's statewide and district candidates.

In order to achieve this goal the county committee:

- Conducts county wide voter registration drives

- Conducts sustained public information programs to sway the voters

- Raises campaign funds and apportions them among local district and state candidates

- Builds the strongest precinct volunteer organization possible to deliver the "friendly votes" on election day

Membership on the county committee varies by state. In some states, the county committee members are elected at specially called meetings (caucuses or conventions). In other states, the county committee members are elected by supervisorial or legislative district, or by precinct. Each district or precinct is allotted a predetermined number of county committee members, based on the voter population within that area.

LOCAL COMMITTEES

In some states, the official party organization structure extends all the way to the local (town or city) level. Such is usually the case where the local officials (city councilmen, mayor, city clerk, etc.) are elected on a partisan basis.

The local party committee is generally composed of the precinct leaders within the town or city. There, precinct leaders are elected by their peers— the registered voters of that party in their precinct. If the precincts are then combined into wards, for organizational or operational purposes, the ward leader becomes a member of the party's town or city executive committee.

THE PRECINCT

The precinct is the vital unit, the cornerstone, of politics. It is *the place of power* for individuals like you. It is the foundation of political organization; *here the party lives or dies, and elections are won or lost.*

Because it is the key to winning elections, all of Chapter Three will be devoted to studying its organization and function.

"UNOFFICIAL" PARTISAN GROUPS

Individual citizens often join together to form "unofficial" partisan political organizations. Often such groups come into being when the official party organization resembles a "closed show" or when the party does not recognize or consider the viewpoint of a large bloc of its constituents.

Sometimes these volunteer, or "unofficial," groups are tied to the candidacy of one person, such as "Citizens for Reagan" or "Citizens for Obama." Others are formed to promote a particular political viewpoint within the party. Generally, those who form or join such organizations are issue-oriented, motivated more by political philosophy and idealism than by personalities or a drive for personal power or prestige. Quite often these groups are successful in swaying the official party organization toward their viewpoint on issues and programs.

Probably the most important activities of the unofficial group are the pre-primary endorsements and election campaign efforts on behalf of its favored candidates. Since the official party generally remains neutral in contested primary elections, the unofficial groups can often have a disproportionate influence on the outcome of those elections.

Generally these volunteer groups cooperate with the regular party organization after the primary and during the general election campaigns. Members of the unofficial groups join in the major voter-registration and get-out-the-vote drives, including special "victory squad" efforts on election day. Republicans tend to have the greater number of volunteer (or unofficial) groups. Democrats traditionally have looked to organized labor and its various political action arms for assistance in voter campaigns and precinct work.

"THIRD FORCE GROUPS"

"Third Force Groups," independently organized and representing special interest groups, attempt to influence political parties by donations and involvement in campaigns. Furthermore, they try to influence the political process through lobbying.

Some of the more prominent and/or powerful third force groups in existence today are:

ACLU—American Civil Liberties Union
ACU—American Conservative Union
ADA—Americans for Democratic Action
AFBF—American Farm Bureau Federation
CWA - Concerned Women for America
COPE—the political action arm of the AFL-CIO
FAMILY RESEARCH ACTION
HERITAGE ACTION
NEA—National Education Association
NRA—National Rifle Association
National Right to Work Committee
Right to Life
NAACP—National Association for the Advancement of Colored

People

Tea Party Organizations (FreedomWorks, et. al)

This is a short list, just to give you an example of the third force groups influencing politics and legislation today. There are many more on the national level as well as on the state and county level. And their influence is extremely great—especially when private individuals like yourself are not involved at all.

To see a more complete list visit:
http://en.wikipedia.org/wiki/List_of_political_action_committees
.

3 THE POWER OF THE PRECINCT

Just as the family is the basic unit of society, so is the precinct the basic unit of politics. The precinct is where the action is—the place where the political party lives or dies, and elections are won or lost. It may be called a precinct, a ward or a voting district. We will use the term "precinct" to represent this political entity.

The precinct is a geographical area arbitrarily drawn by county election officials on the basis of several hundred citizens of voting age. It is your neighborhood! Each political party has volunteer workers. It is their responsibility to contact the voters in that precinct and deliver the "friendly" vote on election day. In some state precinct workers are elected and in others they may be appointed by party leaders.

At the end of Chapter One, you saw how important one vote can be—how candidates for public office won or lost by one vote or less per precinct. That should indicate that a precinct is a critically important—even powerful—place. And in Chapter Two, you looked at the political structure of a political party, seeing that a precinct is the base of power in selecting party leaders. Now we need to take a close look at the structure of the precinct and how it operates, and examine the tools it uses to deliver the winning vote on election day.

STRUCTURE OF A PRECINCT

To repeat: the precinct is *your neighborhood*. It is not some "far away place with a strange sounding name" or populated with strange people living around you in an area that is totally unfamiliar to you. You are on "home ground!" Therefore, structuring your precinct, making it a logical, workable precinct should be relatively easy.

Start by dividing the precinct into blocks formed by roads and streets and their intersections. If a block is heavily populated, you may need to recruit one precinct worker per block; on the other hand, if it is sparsely populated, two or three blocks may be combined into a unit and assigned to a single blockworker or a team, often a husband and wife.

If you were to draw an organizational chart for a typical precinct it would look something like this:

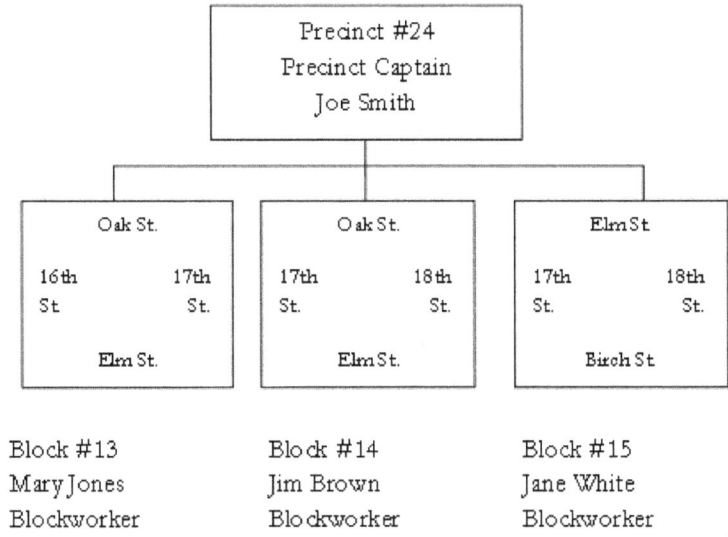

In a map of the county showing precinct boundaries, the precincts will look something like this:

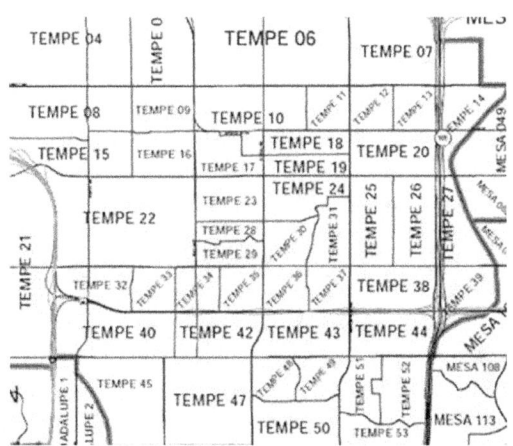

You can divide your precinct into even smaller units on the basis of population—often a single city block. It is an area that one person or a couple can canvass in a reasonable length of time. In a rural area the territory covered would probably be larger, depending on the density of population. The block-worker's area must not be too large in number of households. It must be an area that the worker can handle without too much difficulty.

PARTY ORGANIZATION VS. CAMPAIGN ORGANIZATION

Before we look at the duties of the precinct captain, the committeemen and the block-workers, we need to clarify a point. You may be asking the question, "What is the difference between the party organization and the campaign organization?" Answer: "It depends!" In a primary election, it depends on whether or not the precinct captain and the committeemen are supporting your candidate. If they are, then you recruit them into your own team. If only some of them support your candidate, recruit those and supplement their ranks with volunteers of your own choosing. If none of them do, find yourself a whole new team! This may hold true in the general election, also. If you have some disgruntled committeemen in the party organization—people who worked for the other candidate in the primary election and are not willing to support your candidate, the winner, "no matter what," then simply find someone else. *The point is that you need a precinct captain, precinct committeemen and/or block-workers who hold your political philosophy and support your candidate if you are going to win on election day. Now, let's look at who's who in the precinct.*

THE PRECINCT CAPTAIN

The precinct captain is a key person in your campaign. Abraham Lincoln described his job perfectly when he said:

> *"The whole state must be so well organized that every Whig can be brought to the polls. So divide your county into small districts and appoint in each a committee. Make a perfect list of the voters and ascertain with certainty for whom they will vote. Keep a constant watch on the doubtful voters and have them talked to by those in whom they have the most confidence. On election day see to it that every Whig is brought to the polls."*

It is the job of the precinct captain to head the "committee," to make the "perfect list," to find out how each voter in his precinct intends to vote, to convince the doubtful to vote for your candidate, and to get all the positive votes, the ones for your candidate, to the polls on election day! This is the heart of politics. *This is the secret of winning elections: organizing the precincts—every one of them!*

Because the job of the precinct captain is a critical one, you must choose a person who can get the job done well. He/she must, first of all, be a person who gets along well with people and can motivate them to work for your candidate. He should be interested enough in his neighbors that he can easily recruit a few of them as blockworkers, and he must be able to give them some basic training on how to contact voters in each and every household. He or she needs to be a leader who can keep his workers going enthusiastically even when things get a little tough. And, finally he must be loyal to the candidate and willing to go "the extra mile" in order to win. When you have a man or woman like this to head up each precinct in your election district you have got the election half won.

PRECINCT COMMITTEEMEN AND BLOCKWORKERS

Generally the term "precinct committeeman" applies to those persons who are the official party representatives to that precinct. Prior to an election they may recruit more helpers whom they call "blockworkers." In a campaign precinct organization, it is separate from the official party organization, the precinct worker is usually referred to as a "blockworker" rather than precinct committeeman. We will use the two terms interchangeably—these are the persons who assist the captain in organizing their precinct and identifying the friendly voters.

The blockworkers are found in the area or neighborhood, those neighbors who share your political philosophy and enthusiasm for your candidate. Don't be afraid, however, to educate them first, and then recruit them. Newcomers can add a great deal of enthusiasm and good spirit to a group. Married couples can work as a team, involving their children in the political process as well. Anyone who is able, who is enthusiastic, and who wants to help should be allowed to do so—there is no limit on the number of helpers you can have. A sad commentary on a political organization is the statement by a constituent, "I called the candidate's office and offered to help, but no one ever contacted me!" Don't let that happen in *your* campaign.

PRECINCT TOOLS

Just as a carpenter, an artist, or a draftsman needs tools to work with, so does a precinct worker need special aids. First we will look at the tools used primarily by the precinct captain and then at those used mainly by the committeeman and blockworkers.

Because every precinct worker may not have the equipment or computer skills to do the following work on the computer, the instructions are for manual recording. However all the forms, etc. can be put on a spreadsheet. You are encouraged to utilize the computer as much as possible to make the job easier to perform and the information easier to share. We'll discuss this in more detail later in this chapter in the "Technology" section in Chapters 14 & 18.

Precinct Map

A precinct map shows the boundaries of the precinct and the streets within those boundaries.

If your area chairman does not have such a map to give you, *make your own*. Obtain a map of your precinct, ward or voting district from either the county clerk or elections department. Be sure the map shows the streets. If they do not have a small map of your precinct, draw your own map by hand, showing each street and block within the precinct as well as the outer boundary streets. In most states you will be able to do a Google search for your Congressional district which will show you the areas for the precinct, wards or voting district.

When you have completed mapping the boundaries of your precinct, mount the map on a piece of heavy cardboard and/or tack it on the wall in a prominent place in your work area so you can refer to it easily during the campaign.

Use map pins to show those blocks that are covered by workers. Use *different* colored pins to indicate the blockworkers who are doing a good job, those who are doing a marginal job (and need some motivation) and those who are doing a poor job. (and need to be replaced or assisted). Also designate a color for the area that has *no* worker, reminding you that you need to recruit one

Voter Index List

Registered voter index lists are the large, official sheets of paper on which are printed in alphabetical order or by street the name and address of *every registered* voter in the precinct/district/county. They are prepared and produced by the county clerk or the registrar of voters. These are the same sheets the election workers tack on the wall outside your polling place on election day.

Because ours is such a mobile society, no list is fully accurate—you *must* keep this list up-to-date by getting acquainted with every new family as soon as they move into your precinct area (just watch for the moving vans or "for sale" signs). Welcome them to the neighborhood just as soon as they move in and you will make them your friends. Just as a dull scalpel is of no use to a surgeon, an inaccurate voter index list is of little use to a precinct worker.

In many counties it is possible to get the voter index list in the form of a "walking list;" that is a list of all voters by street and house number in sequence. This enables you to go from door to door, knowing the name and number of people registered in that household. This can be an invaluable aid. But it, too, *definitely must be kept up-to-date by you.*

The "Old Way" is to use Card Files

Card files are to a precinct worker what a hammer is to a carpenter—a tool critical to his success. It is wise to have a "two card file" system—the *house* card file and the *name* card file.

On a 3" x 5" card (or digital version), taking the information from your voter index sheets, make a separate card for each address on every street in your precinct. Print (or type) the street name and house number at the top of the card, and under it, record the *name of each registered voter* listed at that address. File these cards by street name, and then for that street by house number.

A "house card" will look like this:

```
┌──────────────────────────────────────────────┐
│  Oak Street                     #1601          │
│                                                │
│                                                │
│  White, John                                   │
│  White, Isabel                                 │
│  White, John Jr.                               │
└──────────────────────────────────────────────┘
```

The second set of file cards are the *"name cards."* Again using the index of voters, make a file card for each voter at each address.

Record the *name* of the voter at the top of the card, last name first. Under the *name* write the address and phone number. If two or more registered voters with the same last name reside at the address you need only one card, but be sure to list *all voters*. If a person or persons with *different last names* live at the same address (a relative, a renter, etc) *make a separate name card for each individual voter or family.*

File these cards alphabetically by name. If the phone number is not listed on the voter index sheet, have someone in your family look each up for you early in the campaign and record it on the proper card. This way the cards are ready when you need them.

The *"name "* card will look like this:

```
┌──────────────────────────────────────────────┐
│  White, John              480-123-4567         │
│  White,                          Isabel        │
│  White, John Jr.                               │
│                                                │
│                                                │
│  1601 Oak Street                               │
└──────────────────────────────────────────────┘
```

The New Way

You can also do this on a spread sheet that can be sorted by name or by address. It is important to get as much information as you can. Mobile phone numbers and email addresses are perfect contact points to get out the vote on election day. CAUTION: Don't "overuse" them so when you contact your neighbor they willingly open your text message or your email or listen to the voice mail you leave them. See the spread sheet sample here:

Spread Sheet

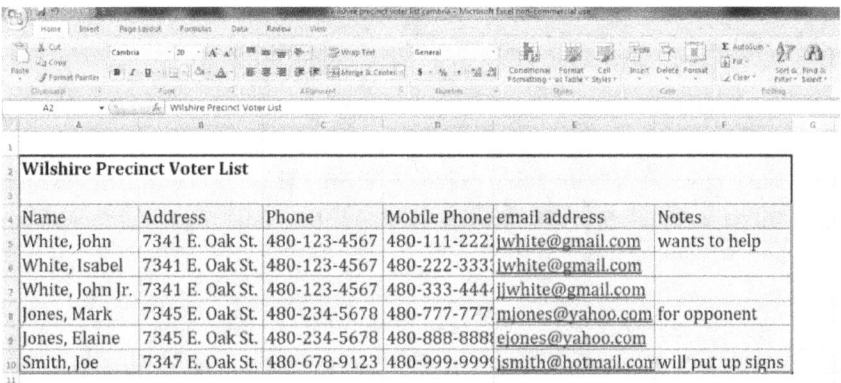

Name	Address	Phone	Mobile Phone	email address	Notes
White, John	7341 E. Oak St.	480-123-4567	480-111-2222	jwhite@gmail.com	wants to help
White, Isabel	7341 E. Oak St.	480-123-4567	480-222-3333	jwhite@gmail.com	
White, John Jr.	7341 E. Oak St.	480-123-4567	480-333-4444	jjwhite@gmail.com	
Jones, Mark	7345 E. Oak St.	480-234-5678	480-777-7777	mjones@yahoo.com	for opponent
Jones, Elaine	7345 E. Oak St.	480-234-5678	480-888-8888	ejones@yahoo.com	
Smith, Joe	7347 E. Oak St.	480-678-9123	480-999-9999	jsmith@hotmail.com	will put up signs

Sometime before primary election—at least three weeks before—the precinct captain should receive the latest voter index sheets from the county elections department or the political party. Using your "name" card file made earlier in the campaign, or your spreadsheet, update your card file against the new index sheet. If there are any voters who died or moved away, mark these on the voter index sheet or spreadsheet. Because the county clerk cannot remove a registered voter's name from the index sheet until and/or unless that voter failed to cast a ballot in the previous general election, you can only rely on the precinct captain's up-to-date card files/spreadsheet to know who is not eligible to vote in that precinct.

Errors in the index sheet should be given to the volunteers who will serve as poll watchers on election day, so that he/she can challenge any person who tries to cast a ballot for a voter who has moved out of the precinct or who has died, etc. The stories you hear about "dead voters" is sadly often true.

Poll watching and challenging the illegal voter is a legal and important way to protect the ballot box from "ghost" voting.

If you cannot get the latest index sheet in time to check it against your card files prior to election day, go to the polls early on that morning and check your card files of dead and moved-away voters against the index sheet that will be posted, by law, near the door of the polling place. There should be no objection to your checking the index sheet as long as you do not interfere with the voting process. Then give those dead or moved away voter cards to your party's "challenger" who will sit at the polling place that day. The poll worker/challenger could also be you.

Blockworker Chart: The "Old Way" and the "New Way"

The blockworker chart, used in conjunction with the precinct map, will give you an immediate awareness of where your workers are, how to reach them, and what kind of job they are doing. You can also tell at a glance which areas need workers. For the precinct captain, the blockworker's chart is an absolutely essential tool.

Setting up the blockworker chart is quite simple. Divide a sheet of typing or tablet paper into four columns. In the left hand column print the heading, "Street and House Numbers;" at the top of the second column type "Blockworker Information;" at the top of the third column print "Blockworker's Address and Phone;" and in the right hand column print the heading "Job Performance." You can, of course, do this in a spreadsheet as well.

Street & House #s	Blockworker Info	Blockworker Contact Info	Job Rating
Elm Street 1600–5299	Bert and Betty Brown bbrown@cox.net	1746 E. Elm St. 480-123-4567 M 480-111-2222	Excellent
16th Street 5200–	Jack and Jeanne Moore jmoore@hotmail.com	5240 N. 16th St. 480-123-1234 M 480-333-4444	Marginal - very slow
17th Street 5200–		5434 N. 17th St. 480-123-4567	Excellent - great recruiter

Spread Sheet

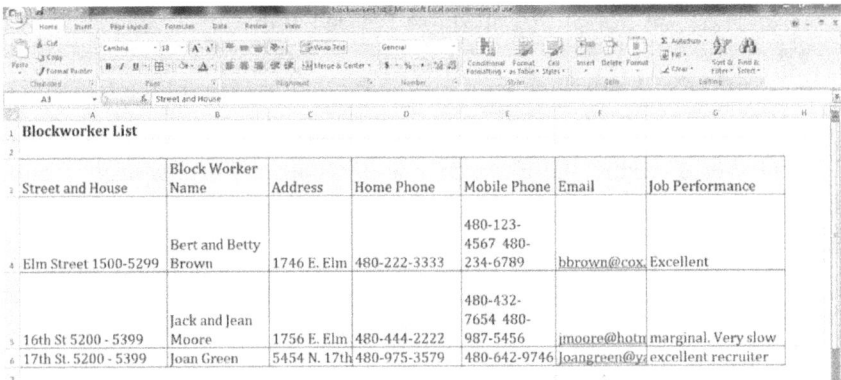

Street and House	Block Worker Name	Address	Home Phone	Mobile Phone	Email	Job Performance
Elm Street 1500-5299	Bert and Betty Brown	1746 E. Elm	480-222-3333	480-123-4567 480-234-6789	bbrown@cox.	Excellent
16th St 5200 - 5399	Jack and Jean Moore	1756 E. Elm	480-444-2222	480-432-7654 480-987-5456	jmoore@hotn	marginal. Very slow
17th St. 5200 - 5399	Joan Green	5454 N. 17th	480-975-3579	480-642-9746	joangreen@yi	excellent recruiter

Obviously there are more sophisticated, online and technological solutions to creating and managing your database on many different levels. We talk more about his in the second half of the book.

Campaign Address Book

The precinct captain should have an address book made up for him/her by the campaign headquarters. It should contain both home and business addresses, land line and mobile phone numbers as well as email addresses of all *key campaign people* at the district, region, and area levels.

City Register

This book contains the names of all members of a family residing at each address in the city. It also lists the occupations of the wage-earners as well as their place of employment. It can be helpful in determining who is unregistered at each home or apartment.

TOOLS FOR THE BLOCKWORKER

The precinct captain should make up a "kit" for each blockworker if that blockworker is to "get off to a good start" and know precisely what is expected of him. A study paper folder with side pockets will do quite nicely to hold the contents of this "kit." If these are not supplied by the campaign headquarters, they can be purchased for a few cents by the captain for his blockworkers.

This can also be sent as a file attachment to the blockworker's email or given to each blockworker on a CD, DVD or USB flash drive.

Following are the "tools" that need to be placed in this kit:

Blockworker's Detail Sheet(or Canvassing Information Sheet)

Very simply, the Blockworker's Detail Sheet is designed for the blockworker to record the vital information about each voter in the house or apartment assigned to him/her. Below is an example of how the detail sheet might look:

ASSIGNED AREA: 16TH Street 5200-5299		
HOUSE #	**VOTER'S NAME**	**COMMENTS**
5200	McCue, John & Sharon	Both registered. GOP. Are committed to our candidate. May volunteer to work in campaign
5201	White, James, Ted, Joan & Jeffry	New in area. Not registered. Prefer only liberal or socialist candidates.
5203	Smith, Gregory, Jim, Shirley	Regis. DEM. Want more information about our candidate

This information recorded in the "Comments" column is very important. It is your key to getting out only the "friendly" the vote on election day. It is up to the blockworker to keep it up-to-date and see that the "needs" recorded in the "Comments" column are taken care of. For example, a person may need a ride to the polls or need a baby-sitter on election day. The blockworker needs to contact either the right people in the campaign headquarters or the precinct driver who will pick them up and drive them to the polls. But, the blockworker must make the need known.

The sheet is turned in to the precinct captain at the completion of each precinct "canvas day" during the campaign. From the information on that sheet, the precinct captain can update the card files or spread sheets. The sheets are then returned to the blockworker for future use. The captain may wish to have a "coffee klatch" during which the blockworkers transfer the information to the card file—this greatly relieves the workload of the captain and can be a motivating "team session" as well.

If you are using computer spreadsheets, be sure to date them each time you submit them. Because they reside in your computer, the precinct captain does not need to return them. (You can still get together for coffee!)

Canvassing Technique Sheet

Old Way

For each precinct activity such as a registration drive, voter canvass, literature drop, etc. a special one-page information sheet should be prepared setting forth the details of the project and the suggested methods to be followed.

These sheets, produced by the region or area leaders, should be distributed to each precinct captain and then to each blockworker. The blockworker should keep such information sheets in the "kit" for ready reference. These technique sheets are quite important because they give the blockworker clear, concise directions regarding the work he is to accomplish in the precinct that day...whether by phone or door to door visits.

New Way If the person doing the canvassing has a tablet computer he can collect and enter the data as he meets people in the precinct. He may be able to do this with a smart phone or iphone as well. The best case scenario is to have tablets or smart phones the blockworkers can take with them and enter the data directly into the computer on software that syncs with the campaign headquarters' database.

Calendar of Campaign Events

Old Way: An absolute "must" in the blockworker's kit is a calendar prepared by the campaign headquarters. It sets forth the major events that have been scheduled throughout the campaign. Every member of the precinct organization must have a copy—in fact, every person working in any capacity in the campaign should have a current copy of the calendar.

New Way: Most campaign headquarters will have a website and an online calendar that you can check on a regular basis from your computer.

You or your precinct captain may wish to set up a Google Calendar that syncs the teams calendars so you can see at a glance what each member of the precinct team has scheduled.

Reverse Telephone Directory

These directories list telephone numbers by street name and house number (and give the subscriber's name). With one of these directories, it takes only a few minutes to list the phone numbers for every house on that block, if the phone numbers are not printed out by the computer on your voter index sheets.

List of Voter Registrars

Check with your county elections office to determine how you help someone register to vote. If you are permitted to register voters be sure you carry the forms you need with you when you canvass the neighborhood.

Be sure you have a list with addresses and phone numbers of those locations where people can register.

No one in your precinct who votes "your way" should be unregistered and uninformed. It's up to you to get the voters that hold your political philosophy registered and let the opposition party worry about getting their supporters registered.

Always be aware that one vote could make the difference.

REMEMBER

It is in the precinct that the right voters are found! The campaign that best organizes their volunteer workers in each precinct and turns out the right-thinking voters in behalf of their candidate are, quite simply, the WINNERS! So, from the first day of the campaign to election day, remember, the precinct is power!

4 THE WINNING CANDIDATE

Think back to the last election. Why did you vote for one candidate rather than the other? Why did you vote for Joe Smith instead of George Jones? Why did you vote for a certain Senate candidate or member of the House of Representatives? Assuming that you are an informed, intelligent voter, you voted for Joe because he best represents YOUR thinking on the issues. He stands for the same things you do—or at least his stand more accurately represents your own than does that of George Jones. Right? Joe will represent YOU. You believe he will vote the way YOU would vote if you were the elected official. He takes your place!

If the elected official is there to represent YOU and others with like minded views then, when selecting a candidate you need to seek out those men and women who can best represent you and others holding your political philosophy. The question is: *Where do you find them and how do you persuade them to become candidates, if a good person is not already in office?*

FINDING A CANDIDATE

Basically, there are three types of persons who run for political office: the statesman, the ambitious, and the special interest representative. The "statesman" agrees to run because he feels a sense of public duty—he believes in the American system of government and wants to do his part to strengthen it. The "ambitious" candidate runs for office because he sees an opportunity for power, fame or financial gain. The "special interest" candidate runs because he is put forth by a special interest faction who wants him to be "their man" in government. Some candidates are a combination of these three motivations. Each could be a good representative, depending on his political philosophy and stand on the issues. Because few candidates are truly "drafted" by their neighbors (the "spontaneous" draft is usually planned and carefully orchestrated by political pros), you need to know how you and your group can find and prepare a winning candidate yourselves.

31

THE SEARCH

As the teacher used to say, "Put on your thinking cap!" Remember those men and women that you have discussed local issues with? What about those who have shared your concern about the direction your state and national government are taking? Have you attended any political seminars or good government conferences in the past few years? If so, who do you know that attended it with you? Write these names down, look up their phone number and give them a call. Get together to discuss the future.

When you are all together and are settled down for serious conversation, remind them about how unhappy they have been with the incumbent, "What's-His-Name." Remind them that the Congressional seat, for example, will be up for grabs next year; or that the state senate seat needs to be occupied by someone who represents the thinking of the constituents for a change; or that the mayor or city councilman is retiring or that half or all of the school board is to be elected next Fall, etc.

Begin enthusiastically, saying, for example, "Here is a great opportunity! Isn't it about time we had someone in that office who believes more in free enterprise and Constitutional government? Wouldn't it be great if we had someone who _____ (put your cause here)" Absolutely!. "Isn't it time we had someone truly concerned with the needs of this area?" Of course it is! And then, give them the challenge: "Why don't *we* find someone to run for the office and then get behind him or her and get him elected? Who can represent us the best?"

Have a "brainstorming" session. Encourage the members of the group to come up with some names. You or several others in the group may already have one or two people in mind. Suggest them to the group, too. Before the time is over, you will probably have suggested several good solid prospects.

It is helpful if your potential candidate for higher office has a record of public service—as a member of a school board, city council, local commission, etc. Or he can be a prominent member of the business or professional community who has devoted time to civic activities. These help to give the candidate some name recognition and provide a better "poll position." However, the individual who has no prior political or civic record should not be overlooked. With Watergate, Billygate, Abscam, Enron, Bill and Monica, the John Edward's affair, Tom DeLay and the other scandals taking place in the realms of government the voters are more interested than ever in a fresh, clean face.

THE ATTRIBUTES OF A GOOD CANDIDATE

The vetting process is critically important and should be done thoroughly and carefully for any possible candidate. We will look at some of the things you need to consider.

There are basically seven requirements of a good candidate for public office which we call the seven Cs:

Clean. Does the individual have any skeletons rattling around in his private or public closet? Anything to be ashamed of? Anything that could flare and cause voter disgust or doubt? In a political campaign you can be sure your past will catch up with you. If he does have indiscretions in his past, can he bring it out himself and survive? Sometimes people overlook those things that you overcome and his life shows that he "learned his lesson" and changed for the better because of it.

Clear. Is the individual articulate? Does he make sense when he speaks? Can he express himself clearly and forcefully? Is he willing and able to say what he means and do it in a convincing and positive manner.

Capable. Does the individual have obvious abilities based on a record of success in private or public life? Has the individual done an outstanding job in some capacity? As chairman of some community effort, as leader in youth work, as a frontrunner in his profession or industry?

Constructive. Does the individual have positive solutions to offer or is he simply a carping critic? Does he offer constructive alternatives? Solid ideas? Does he give reason to believe he can do a better job in office than the other fellow?

Consistent. Not bull-headed but steady. Not wishy-washy, not obnoxious, but firm. One who does not jump from side to side in an effort to curry favor and win voters. Do you know someone like that?

Courageous. Is the individual willing to take a stand and speak out on the issues? Even when the ground is rough and the going gets tough? Is he a leader, a person who inspires others to follow, one in whom the voters will have confidence? Does he convey the image that he will be a fighter for the best interests of his constituents and for the principles in which he believes?

Constitutional. Is the individual a supporter of individual liberty, Constitutional government, competitive free enterprise, and fiscal responsibility?

GOOD HEALTH AND STAMINA

Campaigns can be compared to the Boston Marathon in terms of the need of good health and stamina.

It is most likely that your candidate will not be wealthy nor will he be backed by "big money." This means that your candidate will have to get out and "sell" himself to the voters—he will have to talk to them in order to win their support and votes. To do this he has to go where the voters are—to shopping centers, to their homes, to rallies, etc, and this takes energy and endurance. Be sure he has it.

A CANDIDATE CECKLIST

Knowing the traits you and your group have in mind for your candidate you need to make up a checklist—a yardstick by which to measure his strengths and weaknesses. Give points—perhaps a scale of one to five—and have each person in your group rate each trait listed. Have a pre-established standard of grading his acceptability so you can assess whether or not he meets your standards. Do this for each potential candidate.

The following checklist or "Candidate Analysis" can also be used in evaluating any candidate for any elected office.

CANDIDATE ANALYSIS

District _____

State _____

Name _____

Address _____

POLITICAL YARDSTICK

Reputation   _____

Qualified for Office   _____

Experienced in campaigning   _____

Physical appearance   _____

Personality   _____

Really wants the job   _____

Active in community affairs   _____

Record as prior candidate   _____

Name familiar to voters   _____

Appeal to independent voters   _____

Press relations   _____

Platform performance   _____

Television performance   _____

Radio voice   _____

Military record   _____

Athletic record   _____

Fraternal affiliations   _____

Smaller "organized groups" support   _____

Position on issues   _____

Aggressive campaigner   _____

Personal financial ability to run   _____

Capability of raising campaign funds   _____

Party support _____

TOTAL POINTS _____

HOW TO SCORE EACH POLITICAL FACTOR	HOW TO EVALUATE TOTAL SCORE
5 Excellent	95+ Excellent candidate
4 Above average	70-94 Good candidate
3 Average	55-70 Fair candidate
2 Fair	54 or below. Poor candidate
1 Poor	

CANDIDATE INTERVIEW QUESTIONNAIRE

Now that you have "weeded out" the candidates who don't meet your standards, you need to meet with the finalists to determine their stand on the issues, to see how they perform under pressure, to find out if they are interested in being a candidate, etc. But *before* you meet with each one, you need to *prepare*—to devise an interview guide to insure an intelligent, comprehensive interview. Otherwise, you are wasting your time as well as the potential candidate's time.

In preparing the questionnaire, first list the *important public issues* and then arrange them in order of importance so that you cover the most important one first. Be sure to include only those issues that apply to the level of government for which the person is being considered. For example, you would not quiz a possible mayoral candidate about national defense issues, nor would you ask a candidate for school board about his stand on State highway spending.

SAMPLE CANDIDATE QUESTIONNAIRE FOR SENATE OR CONGRESSIONAL SEAT

Get some short form answers to the top issues concerning your base. For example:

1. Please describe your position on National Defense?

2. What is your position on Obamacare?

3. What is your solution to the immigration problem?

4. What tax reform changes would you support?

5. What is your plan for improving education?

6. What changes in the law would you propose for reducing the regulations burdening small businesses and homeowners?

7. What is your position on Foreign Policy?

Personal Information

Name _____

Address: Street_____

City _____State_____ Zip_____

Precinct _____

Business Phone _____Home_____

Cell_____

Type of employment _____

Birth date _____ Birthplace _____

Spouse's name _____

Spouse's employment _____

Names and ages of children _____

_____

_____

Party affiliation _____

Office being sought_____

Please attach a summary of 1) Education; 2) employment background; 3) community and political involvement.

● ● ●

The questionnaire you draft should be tailored to suit an individual campaign at any level of the political spectrum and according to your policy interests.

CONDUCTING THE INTERVIEW

Now it is time to see your potential candidate in person! You and two or three members of the group need to contact each of the individuals on your list of potential candidates. Set up a meeting with each of them so you can determine if he or she is interested and willing to run for the office. If they don't give you an absolute and emphatic "no," go through the candidate questionnaire with him/her. (And don't take the first "no" for a final answer. Sometimes the best candidate—the one who wins—is the one who is the most reluctant in the beginning).

After each candidate is interviewed, set up a meeting with the entire membership of your group to meet the acceptable candidates. Let other members of the group ask questions—any questions, as long as they are relevant and pertain to the office for which he is being considered. It is better to ask the questions now than to find out later—after the campaign gets under way—that "undiscovered" information can be damaging to your candidate. Remember the damage done to Thomas Eagleton in the 1972 McGovern-Eagleton campaign for the presidency and vice presidency? No one asked Eagleton if he had ever been under the care of a psychiatrist, and he did not consider the information to be important. However, the press did and his credibility was questioned until he withdrew his candidacy. Don't let that happen to your candidate.

In 1987 married former Senator Gary Hart announced the beginning of his second Presidential campaign. Less than a month later, the *Miami Herald* published a photo of a young woman leaving Hart's residence. They then published photos showing a 29-year-old model, Donna Rice, sitting on

Hart's lap. Less than a week later, Hart announced he was dropping out of the race. We've already talked about John Edwards. These kinds of skeletons can't be put back into the closet and once the public feels deceived there is generally no turning back. He will most likely be forced to withdraw to his detriment and your loss of credibility.

After you have interviewed each potential candidate, your committee needs to get together, rating sheets in hand and scores tallied, and make a decision about who is the most electable. Once that decision is made, it is time to meet again with him (or her) and help him decide to *be* the candidate, to persuade him that the election can be won with him as candidate—and you and your group as knowledgeable and willing workers behind him.

Does this sound too easy? Basically, this is the process followed in selecting candidates at every level of government. Many men and women are in office today, from school boards to the United States Congress because two or three people got behind them encouraging them to run and backing them up with intelligent volunteer efforts.

But, one thing you do need to consider: in the event that some other people with like principles as you come up with a candidate, get both groups together and try to agree on one candidate for each office. Don't risk losing the election by splitting those who vote for YOUR candidates into two camps and letting the opposition elect their *one* candidate! Keep egos out of it.

Now you have chosen your one candidate and he has agreed to run. Let's get on with the business of building the candidate—helping him become a winner at the polls on election day!

THE BUILDING OF THE CANDIDATE

In building your candidate, you must first of all sit down and make a plan—a plan for presenting your candidate to the public in the most positive way. To devise a workable, meaningful plan you need to objectively look at your candidate, assess the issues and targets and most likely do some surveys or polls. Let's take a look at each of these.

THE CANDIDATE

You have chosen your candidate because he has certain strengths, abilities, a public or civic record or a combination of these. You already have someone you think the public will like and, hopefully, vote for on election day. But now you need to take a more critical look in order to determine the strengths the public will "buy" and the weaker attributes that need to be minimized.

THE CANDIDATE'S PERSONALITY

Assuming that he already possesses the seven C's (clean, clear, capable, constructive, consistent, courageous and Constitutionally oriented) you need to think about his personality. In what type of setting does he really shine? Is he great before a large audience or does he function best in small informal groups? Is he an excellent speaker, a real dynamo on the platform? Or does he get a bad case of stage fright and have to read his speech word-for-word? Is he super in give-and-take discussion groups or does he give "off-the-cuff" answers that get him in trouble? How is he on a panel? In talk shows? Coffee hours and socials? Some candidates do best shaking hands and greeting people one-on-one. Others can't think of a thing to say in this situation, but are great before large audiences.

Once you know his strengths and weaknesses you can plan a schedule for his public appearances capitalizing on his abilities and avoiding those situations that spotlight his weaknesses. For example, if he is a good speaker, try to get appearances before the service clubs, church groups, civic organizations, community meetings, political groups, etc. Most of these groups look for speakers on a regular basis and will most likely be delighted to have some "new talent" on the scene. Schedule your candidate for as many of these as possible if he presents himself well. If he does better with smaller groups, set up a number of neighborhood coffees, receptions, etc. Try to get him included on as many panels, radio talk shows and discussion groups as you can *before* he announces his candidacy, so he can reach larger groups without having to give "equal time" to his opponent. These contacts increase his name identification before the "formal" phase of the campaign actually begins.

THE CANDIDATE'S RECORD

Assess the candidate's record of achievement and service in local community or public affairs—if not in politics and government, in other areas. List those accomplishments briefly but clearly. Include any civic or service or special awards for outstanding achievement. List memberships and past or present offices in service groups: civic, community, professional, church, military and other patriotic organizations. This is important because each of these groups has its own following, i.e., voters.

When you put this data on a fact sheet, together with a short resume of his personal background (age, marital status, number of children, education, present occupation, etc.) you have the information needed for press releases, brochures and other graphics. It is very wise to compile this early and put it in a file along with some good photographs (head shots) so that you are ready whenever an opportunity for some publicity presents itself.

You will also need a campaign website that is professionally built to feature your candidate and give the public access to information and the schedule. Find someone in the campaign who can keep it up-to-date in order to keep people returning to find out what's happening in the campaign.

Check out Chapter 12, "Website and Search Engine Optimization" for more information about your candidate's web presence.

AREA OF EXPERTISE

What is the candidate's area of expertise? What does he/she know the most about? Where has he had the most experience? What can he talk about most fluently? Whatever it is—education, working with youth, economics, agriculture, law—use the strength to the best advantage. Tie it and the candidate to the important issues of the area or district and to items of interest and concern in the community. Develop your campaign theme or emphasis around it. Keep making the point that "*Here is a person who really can be of important service to us and to the community. We need a person with just these talents.*"

WHAT ABOUT THE OPPONENT

Although some professional campaign managers think that the campaign strategy must have both positive and negative aspects, that may not necessarily be true. Most people want to see a clean, honest, positive campaign. They are tired of "back room deals" and mudslinging. They are looking for men and women who stand *for something* rather than *against someone*.

While the 2012 campaigns, from local to Presidential seemed to be built on negative attack, that doesn't mean it is the best strategy. Ask your neighbors what they think about such tactics. Most of them will say they are tired of it as well as disgusted.

There are some genuine differences in the political philosophy, the stand on issues, the voting record between your candidate and his opponent. This is what you point out. Research the opponent's record—his votes, speeches, public proposals, bills he sponsored, etc. This will help articulate the differences between the two candidates and will sharpen your candidate's own stand. You may find that as the campaign develops, your opponent changes his stand on an issue or makes a contradictory statement. Capitalize on this, but *don't attack him as a person if you can avoid it.*

George Bernard Shaw once stated "I learned long ago, never to wrestle with a pig. You get dirty, and besides, the pig likes it." Negative campaigning can be a drain on your resources, and more importantly on your long term image. Avoid it if possible.

ISSUES AND TARGETS

One of the hardest jobs in a campaign is to get the attention of the voters and maintain their interest. Therefore, it is of greatest importance for you to know what they are interested in and concerned about. If your candidate knows the concerns of the majority and is able to offer realistic and workable solutions rather than empty campaign promises, he will be able to get the ear of the public.

So one of the real questions in the campaign is, "*What are the issues of real concern to the voters in the district?*" There may be a number of closely related issues voiced as a single concern. For example, the economy. Issues clustered around the economy are the high cost of living, heavy taxation, the excessive cost of government, high interest rates, joblessness, a crash in real estate, etc. Other concerns may be related to the increasing amount of government interference in our lives seen in excessive regulations in the work place, government controls in education—private and public, regulations affecting family living such as legislation favoring child advocacy, etc. It is important to know which issues are important in your district if he is to get the voter's attention. *Beware.* He should take a stand and not follow every poll that comes out with different results.

It is also important to know what major voting blocs are within your district that would warrant special attention on the part of the candidate. This may mean ethnic, religious and economic blocs, but it can mean *issue blocs* as well. For example, the Pro-Life/Anti-abortion bloc or the Pro-Choice/Pro-Abortion bloc in the district; the gun control or the anti-gun control blocs; the inflation-fighters bloc, etc. Each of these blocs will be looking for answers to their specific questions about your candidate's stand on issues affecting them and they deserve a straight and honest answer.

Many times you know what the people consider the major issues because you share their concerns and see the same problems. However, that isn't accurate enough to build a campaign strategy on. You have to be more accurate than that. You need to feel the pulse of the district by using *motivational research*. This is simply a public opinion survey or market research—what most of us call a *public opinion poll*.

Firms such as CampaignGrid (http://campaigngrid.com) have extremely detailed and accurate demographic information and targeting services that can help you maximize your time and resources on properly targeted issue oriented voters.

MOTIVATIONAL RESEARCH/PUBLIC OPINION POLLS

Many people, even some who are political veterans, have the idea that a poll shows only who is ahead in the race—your candidate or his opponent. That is one very important aspect of political polling, but not the only one. A critical area of information gleaned by public surveys is what the people perceive as key issues. What are they *worried about* in the community, in the district, in the government at every level?. What areas of concern generate the most emotion and the most fear? What do people see as possible solutions? It can show you what traits they most want to see in their elected officials and which candidates they perceive have those traits. A poll can show you *emerging issues or changes* in the way the voters perceive your candidate.

Because it is critical to a campaign to know these things, research should be placed high on the priority list both in the budget and in the strategy. In a larger campaign—for a state-wide office or for a Congressional district or the state legislature—research should be approximately 10 percent of the total budget. Enough funding should be provided to do a series of polls starting in the early stages of the campaign, and repeated periodically with the final survey taken during the final weeks of the campaign. This keeps the campaign manager and candidate informed of any shifts in public opinion and abreast of any emerging issues.

In a smaller campaign with limited funds the services of a professional research team may not be within the budget, but opinion surveys are still a must. You should try to join with another compatible and non-competing candidate to finance a joint survey or you can conduct your own survey using volunteers. A poll in conjunction with others may not be as personalized and a survey done by volunteers may not be as scientific, but it will provide you with valuable information for the campaign just the same.

Keeping abreast of public opinion does not mean that the candidate changes his stand on the issues in order to tell the public what he thinks they want to hear in order to get their votes. It *does* mean that he can intelligently plan his approach and not stumble blindly into a political hornet's nest. It means that he can base his campaign strategy on voter opinion research rather than on pure guess. This is done not to compromise, but to strategize. According to a veteran campaigner, *"When you compromise, you change your principles; when you strategize, you change your tactics."* Think about the difference!

Now that we have selected our candidate, know his talents and weaknesses, and know how to identify the key issues and targets, it is time to take a look at who we need on the campaign team. A candidate does not run alone—he is accompanied by a team that can help bring about the victory on election day.

5 THE WINNING TEAM

The football team going to the Super Bowl needs a great quarterback, but the quarterback cannot win the game alone—he needs the team! And the rest of the team must be in condition, must know the plays, must feel the cohesiveness of the group, must be ready to give everything they've got to win the victory! They go out on the field as a team and as a team they win or lose. The quarterback may get the spotlight, the praise and adulation of the crowd, but he and everyone else knows that he could never have done it alone.

It was the *team* that won!

The quarterback in a political campaign is the candidate. But he can't get the victory without a winning team to run interference, to "receive the ball" and run with it, to minimize or stop the progress of the opposition. The candidate needs a team to help raise funds, to recruit, train and direct volunteers—in short, to run the daily affairs of the campaign so the candidate has time to be the candidate! This team is called the campaign organization! Let's take a look at how a campaign organization is set up and how it functions so we can build this winning team for our candidate.

Looking at the following diagram entitled "Typical Campaign Organization" you will see that the candidate is the head of the campaign organization. It is official that he is aware of all activities taking place in his behalf, that he has constant input into the campaign, that he is, in essence, "in charge," However, he cannot be responsible for the "nitty gritty" details. He simply does not have the time nor the energy (not enough hours in the day) to be anything but the candidate. While he is out front meeting people, making speeches, giving interviews, someone must be in the background taking care of the details of the campaign. That person is the campaign manager or chairman

CAMPAIGN MANAGER

The campaign manager or chairman is the person who "gets it all together." In concert with the candidate he sets the tone of the campaign, sets up the momentum, and sees that things get done—on time. Together with the candidate, he will help select all other members of the campaign team and help plan the campaign strategy; therefore, it is important that his appointment be made first.

In selecting the campaign manager, it is essential that you look for a man or woman with administrative ability—one who is able to make decisions, to set priorities, and to delegate responsibilities. If at all possible, he should have had previous campaign experience; however, if a professional campaign consultant or manager is hired, this may not be critical. He absolutely must be able to get along with other people—to inspire confidence, to excite them about the candidate and the campaign, and to get them to work together as a team. And, finally, he should be a person who is known and respected in the community. He should know where the talent is and where he can find people who can and will support the campaign with both time and finances.

CAMPAIGN COORDINATOR

If it is a large campaign you may need a campaign coordinator—a person to be the chairman's right hand. If the chairman is a man it is a good idea to have a woman in this position and *vice versa*. This insures a representation of both men and women in the top echelons of the campaign organization, assuring that both points of view will be expressed.

Basically, the Coordinator should have the same qualifications as the Campaign Chairman, especially in the arena of campaign experience. Generally the Coordinator is responsible for the activities of the various subcommittees, leaving the chairman free to work more intensely with the candidate on planning, strategy, timing and fund-raising.

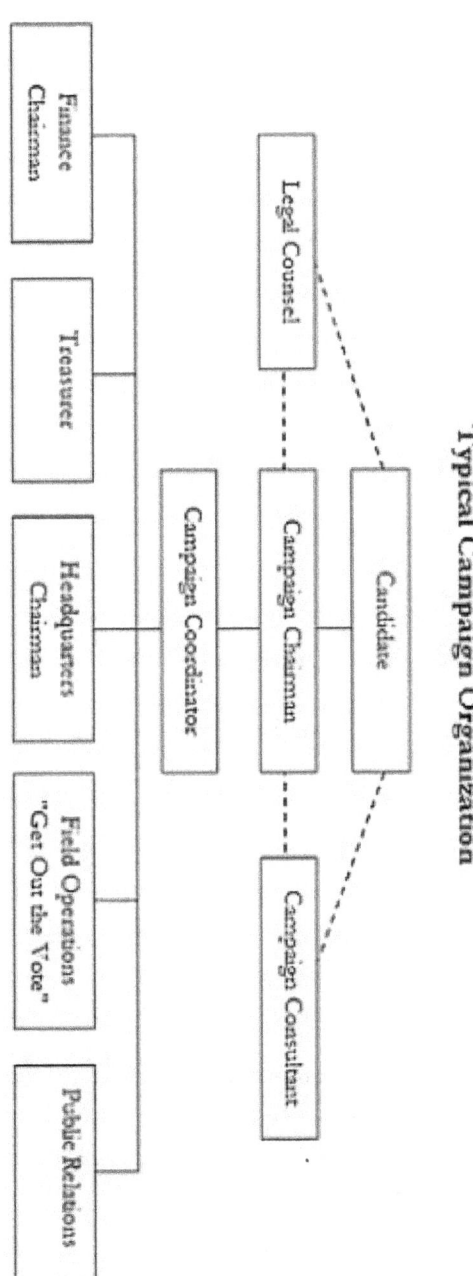

Typical Campaign Organization

FINANCE CHAIRMAN

Every political campaign must have money! This is the chief function of the finance chairman—to be a fund raiser. He does not dispense it! He is not the comptroller! He is not the treasurer! *He raises funds!*

One of the basic qualifications of the Finance Chairman is that he be a leading citizen—in terms of the respect he gets from other community leaders, his financial standing, his community involvement. He should be able to expect other persons of importance and financial ability to accept invitations to fund raisers just because of who he is, and he should have some facility in raising small gifts from people. He should, furthermore, be able to enlist others for his finance committee in every financial bracket, geographical area, profession, industry, throughout the election district. He needs others to help him in the fund raising and he needs to be a man who can get them excited about contributing to the worthwhile campaign of this extraordinary candidate. Finally, he should be a major contributor of the campaign himself. After all, he cannot expect others to give to a campaign he himself is not totally committed to with his own finances and time.

TREASURER

Because all campaign expenditures and receipts are handled by the treasurer, it is critical that this position be handled by a certified public accountant or at least by someone who has a solid background in accounting. It is absolutely necessary to be assured about his honesty—*if you cannot trust him implicitly, don't put him on your campaign staff.*

His responsibilities include:

Keeping the campaign books. All campaign receipts and expenditures should go to the treasurer. No one else in the campaign should handle any of them—ever! This way he can keep the books accurate and up-to-date.

Filing the financial statements required by state and federal law. As more detailed and complex reports are required on both a state and federal level, it is critical that one person—the treasurer—have this under control. An official report, filed inaccurately or after the deadline could disqualify your candidate, even if he wins the election.

Acknowledging all campaign contributions. Because he is handling all income, it is essential that he be responsible for seeing that the "thank yous" get written. They are of utmost importance to the candidate. Even the contributor of the smallest amount is thrilled by a warm, sincere "Thank You" on behalf of the candidate and will often intensify his efforts in the campaign because of it. On the other hand, an unacknowledged contribution can develop a negative attitude toward the candidate and, if the disgruntled contributor does not harm the campaign, he may at least withdraw his further support and/or efforts. This should never be allowed to happen.

Assists in drafting the campaign budget and seeing that the costs do not exceed the cash!

Pays all bills and handles payroll if there is any paid campaign staff.

HEADQUARTERS CHAIRMAN

The Headquarters Chairman is a vital person in the campaign, often being the one who represents the candidate to the general public who may stop in, and certainly representing the candidate to the volunteers who come to help.

This person must be able to manage an office; find, train, motivate and supervise volunteers; keep a supply of necessary materials; oversee the candidate's schedule, supervise the telephone committee; get the literature/mailings out on time; and keep the tone of the headquarters on a positive and enthusiastic level.

The headquarters chairman cannot do the job all by herself. It will probably be necessary to assign others as "day chairman," to find volunteers who can help with the correspondence and telephoning, etc. The real challenge is to keep the volunteers busy, motivated and excited about the campaign.

FIELD OPERATIONS—GET OUT THE VOTE CHAIRMAN

The Field Operations Chairman is responsible for those activities that take place outside the headquarters, particularly in the precincts. Basically, this person is responsible for:

- Recruiting and training precinct workers so that all precincts are well staffed with workers who are for *your* candidate.

- Assuring that the precinct captains and workers are on schedule in completing their registration, voter canvassing, literature drops and get-out-the-vote drives.
- Supplying the precinct workers with campaign materials.
- Acting as communicator between the campaign chairman and the precinct in order that the precinct workers know the "plan of action" and the campaign chairman gets feedback from the people working on the precinct level.
- Assisting in compiling the district's vote profile, i.e., knowing what percentage of the votes in that district need to go to your candidate on a precinct by precinct basis.

Because the precinct is the "winning place"—the most important area of the campaign—the man or woman who fills the position of Field Coordinator must know the political ropes. He needs to have a working knowledge of precinct politics and have a record indicating he knows how to organize a "winning precinct." He must know how to find, recruit, train, motivate and supervise precinct workers—an enormous but highly rewarding job. On election day the Field Operations Chairman can see the fruits of his labor precinct by precinct as the voters come in.

PUBLIC RELATIONS CHAIRMAN

Basically, the Public Relations Chairman has the job of getting your candidate before the public eye in a positive way as often and as inexpensively as possible. In these multi-media times, many candidates choose a highly qualified and respected public relations firm to handle this area. Working closely with the candidate and the campaign chairman, the public relations personnel are responsible for:

- The preparation and production of all campaign materials, including folders, flyers, brochures, bumper stickers, posters, billboards, etc.
- Helping draft the candidate's speeches, statements and position papers on the issues.
- With the candidate's approval, writes and distributes all press releases. Works with the press in building a good professional relationship. If the press likes and respects your P.R. staff and sees

a consistent, high quality job done, they will be much more sympathetic to your candidate. Any advantage in getting good news coverage and other attention in the media is a big boost to the campaign.

- Assists in the design, content, preparation, production and placement of all advertising materials—written, graphic, printed, on line or by mobile phone.

- Prepare and has available to the press a biography of the candidate, a background sheet and a fact file. Has an official campaign photograph done and keeps a file of photos on hand for the use with press releases, etc. Produces a "press kit" and any other materials that may be needed by the press or by those preparing any special campaign newspapers or newsletters in print or digital media.

- Helps the campaign chairman and candidate interpret and assess the findings of polls and surveys and translate these into press releases, speeches, etc.

As you can readily see, the position of Public Relations Chairman is one that requires a great deal of time, tremendous talent and a winning way with people, especially people in the news media. You must have a person who can sell your candidate to the press, who knows journalism and advertising and who can work under great pressure without "losing his cool." Either a full time public relations director should be hired and given adequate staff assistance or your account should be given to a competent and respected public relations firm.

IT DIRECTOR OR "UBER NERD"

Depending upon the size of your campaign and budget you will need an Uber Nerd—Your guru of all things nerdy and computer related. This is a good time to start listening to your children! They know about these things.

Your Uber Nerd can range from your teenage kid, or younger—your first offensive coordinator—to a highly paid consultant who can manage your web site and other digital devices.

If you have the money you can hire a firm like CampaignGrid to figure it all out and run it for you. If you have limited funding, get a firm like them to consult. If you basically have only your personal money, reach out to the party or get your own team of "experts" from church, little league, the neighborhood or wherever you are congregating.

In the end, your "team of experts" will probably win out. That proposition really depends on the excitement you can bring to your candidacy or campaign.

OTHER POSITIONS

We have looked at the key positions in any campaign, positions that will insure that the major needs of the campaign will be met. In a small campaign, say that of school board, one person may be able to fill one or more of the positions. In a large campaign, a state wide race for Governor or United States Senator, for example, you may need to expand each position and create a number of additional committees to insure that "all bases are covered." Some other committees you may need are:

Materials Chairman

This person works closely with the headquarters chairman in seeing that all the equipment and supplies needed during the campaign are on hand at the time they are needed. These materials generally are included in one of the following groups:

- Office equipment, furniture and machines—desks, chairs, work tables, computers, postage scales, etc.
- Basic office supplies—paper, pencils, paper clips, rubber bands, etc.
- Special campaign materials—campaign literature, bumper stickers, buttons, position papers, posters, etc.

For a list of basic supplies needed, see the next chapter on "The Campaign Headquarters."

Special Events Chairman

The stereotype of a political campaign has the candidate kissing babies at the barbecue or shaking hands with everyone he meets at a "town picnic." This is the "fun" part of the campaign, the type of function that makes everyone feel a part of the team. This is a time that the real campaign team can gather up those on the fringe and get them to "jump on the bandwagon." Some of the events that can be planned are:

Picnic, barbecues, spaghetti feeds or watermelon busts for both the precinct workers and the public.

A kick-off rally or dinner that serves as both a time the candidate announces the start of his campaign and as a fund raiser.

Rallies for precinct workers to keep them excited about the campaign, informed about what is happening and motivated to intensify their efforts.

Fund raising buffets or dinners should be planned to reach those who can afford $25.00 to $100 or more a plate for your candidate as well as those who can afford from $5.00 to $20.00 for a potluck or box-lunch affair. It is important to get as many people involved as possible.

Victory Squad Chairman

Comprised generally of individuals who want to help part time in the campaign, victory squads are used to strengthen the precinct organization in areas that are not fully manned. They are used for special precincts such as voter canvassing, registration drives and get-out-the-vote campaigns on election day.

The chairman of this committee should be someone who knows how to find and recruit volunteers. That means he or she should have wide contacts with civic and social groups, churches, colleges, service clubs, etc. The wider his contacts, the more volunteers he is likely to find. Ideally, if volunteers are recruited earlier in the campaign they should be integrated into your precinct organization. Victory squads are mostly last minute volunteers who are put into the weak spots in your organization at the last minute—sort of "roving commandos."

Special Committees

A good campaign strategy used to gain publicity and convey strength is the formation of special committees that endorse your candidate. Such as:

Any profession or special interest group may want to form such a group, e.g., senior citizens, sportsmen, doctors, youth, veterans, clergyman.

Teachers for Jones	Farmers for Jones
Business People for Jones	Pilots for Jones
Nurses for Jones	Lawyers for Jones

The purpose of these groups is general is:

- to provide additional opportunity for publicity;

- to gain additional attention and support for the candidate among various professional, trade and vocational groups; and

- to generate another source of campaign contributions.

Generally, these are "letterhead" committees; that is, a group that depends primarily on mailings to garner support for the candidate and to secure campaign contributions. Usually, a chairman, a co-chairman and a sponsoring board is formed and a letterhead containing these names is printed (generally paid for by the committee members). A letter on this special stationary is sent out to every member of the profession or special interest group announcing the committee's support of your candidate and encouraging every member of the group to throw their support to him also. Included in this mailing are a return envelope and endorsement card, with a request for a financial contribution. The endorsement card should contain a statement that the endorser's name may be used in campaign publicity, such as newspaper advertisements, etc.

The person holding the position of special committee chairman should know people in various professions and special interest groups, and be able to motivate them to form committees and reach members of their own groups. He should be able to assist them in writing the letters and getting the mailings out.

REMEMBER—IT'S A TEAM!

Never, ever forget that it's a team effort and it takes every one working together to get the candidate elected. Remember the goal—victory at the polls on election day.

6 THE CAMPAIGN HEADQUARTERS

The Campaign Headquarters can set the tone for the campaign—it can be a place where volunteers love to come because it is attractive and the people are friendly and dedicated to the candidate. Or it can influence volunteers to stay home and workers not to do their best job. Where it is, how big or small it is, how it is staffed, equipped and supplied, and how it is decorated all affect the quality of work that is done there. Let's take a look at these factors plus a few more.

LOCATION

Basically, the headquarters should be in a safe, convenient location with plenty of parking space. Although it does not have to be "downtown," a location with high street traffic visibility is desirable. This also makes it more likely that public transportation is available, making it possible for volunteers with and without cars to get there.

It does not have to be the fanciest place in town but it should at least be safe. It definitely should not be a fire trap or an eyesore. It should have good light, good ventilation and good heating and cooling.

SIZE

The size depends on the extent of your campaign—a state-wide race requires more space than a local or district race, generally speaking.

A vacant store makes the ideal campaign headquarters. At times an empty home will do if it is large enough and has several big rooms for work areas.

Basically, a headquarters needs several rooms (private or semi-private) for offices, a reception area and a large work space. The candidate, the campaign chairman and the manager should have private offices in order to make phone calls, host small meetings and be able to have quiet time to think and plan.

The work area for preparing mailings, etc., needs to be located away from the hustle and bustle of the reception area and should be arranged to keep distractions at a minimum. It should also be set up so that it can be used as a meeting room when needed.

You will also need plenty of space for storage—you need to store supplies, campaign brochures, yard signs, etc. so that they can be readily accessible and yet not in the way. You don't want your volunteers climbing over boxes of material to get to the work table.

DECORATING THE HEADQUARTERS

The headquarters should "sell" your candidate. It should be bright and attractive, with lots of material related to the candidate.

Outside use big signs along the front and sides of the building identifying it a "So-and-so for Senate" (or whatever) Headquarters. Be sure the sign is attractive and readable—a sign that looks good but cannot be easily read is absolutely worthless and gives your candidate a bad image. If a billboard is nearby, rent that space and put up one of the candidate's billboards.

Decorate the headquarters with the campaign colors—those colors used on the billboards, brochures and bumper stickers: the cumulative effect of repetition will work for you.

It is most important to keep the grounds around the building and the parking lot clean—it makes a better impression on behalf of your candidate.

DECORATING INSIDE

If your headquarters has large display windows, use them to their fullest potential. Use giant posters of your candidate, colored streamers and backdrops, artistic arrangements of campaign materials. Depending on the size of the window, you may want to include blown up pictures and news stories favorable to your candidate, etc. Make the window work for you. Make it so attractive that people want to come in to see what is going on or to see what the inside looks like. After all, if the window is so attractive the interior might be exciting, too.

If the interior is dull and drab, with paint peeling and/or cracked, you might want to do a quick paint job, if the landlord is willing. Teen boys and some of the men generally readily volunteer to do this and have it done in record time. And probably either the landlord or the volunteers would supply the paint. Check this out before you move the furniture in. Be sure to use light colors that are cheery but not glaring—you want a room that makes people feel like working, not one that depresses them and makes them want to get out and go home.

In the reception area use campaign posters and other campaign materials such as yard signs, large pictures of the candidate, other attractive material that may be available. Display the American flag prominently—and the state flag if you have one. Put a large map or maps of the district on one wall and posters highlighting the candidate's stand on key issues on another wall.

If there is a campaign slogan, have this painted on a large banner and hang the banner in the most prominent place. This adds pizzazz to the office.

If there is enough room, have plenty of campaign literature available. This should include brochures, bumper stickers, position papers on key issues, pins with the candidate's name and/or slogan and any other material that may be available.

RENT

The headquarters chairman and/or the general chairman should speak to any realtors who are friendly to the candidate—they may be happy to donate their time and effort to find a suitable facility and may talk to the owner about a "break" in the monthly price.

If you do your job thoroughly you might even find a landlord or realtor who will let you have a good location without charge or at a rate that jut covers utilities, taxes, and insurance. You may have to agree to move if the location is rented, but it is worth the risk.

INSURANCE

Before you move one piece of furniture into the office, find your friendly insurance man (one who supports your candidate) and let him take care of liability insurance for the committee. In some states this type of insurance is called "Owners Landlords and Tenants" liability insurance. No matter what it is called in your state, be sure you are fully insured for the duration of the campaign.

SAFETY AND SECURITY

Your building must be safe! A serious accident or disaster could ruin all your campaign efforts.

First of all, ask the local fire department to inspect the premises. Are there enough fire exits? Are fire extinguishers placed in appropriate places? Are there any hazardous conditions anywhere in the headquarters? These problems must be taken care of *before the headquarters is opened.*

Be sure that there are secure locks on all the doors and windows and have the old locks changed and new keys made. The headquarters must be secure for the safety of the workers and the security of the campaign files.

You should have at least one fireproof, locked file to contain all confidential campaign materials and campaign contributions. (Funds should be banked daily; however, you should have a safe place to store them before banking and a safe place for petty cash.)

TELEPHONES

Land Line Phones

Telephones are one of the most important items in the campaign so be sure you make arrangements enough in advance to have them installed as soon as the headquarters can accommodate them. Reserve your telephone numbers and set a date for installation as soon as you know the location of the building.

Make an efficient survey of need at the beginning so that you order an adequate number of phones and have them placed in the locations that will offer the most efficient use. And be sure that your phone lines are in rotary—so that the incoming calls will automatically switch from one line to the next if the first numbers are busy.

When you assess your needs for telephones, be sure to include one at the reception desk, one in the candidate's office, one in the chairman's office, and one at each of the desks for subcommittee chairmen who work at the headquarters.

The candidate and campaign chairman and probably the finance chairman, should have private *unlisted* numbers in addition to the regular headquarters lines.

If you plan to have a phone bank in the headquarters, you need to plan ahead and have them ordered well in advance. Otherwise, your telephone canvassing, polling, etc. may be delayed to the great detriment of the campaign. You can have them installed just before you need to do the polling, etc., and have them removed when the project is completed BUT order them early.

Cell (Mobile) Phones/Smart Phones

Contact the various mobile phone companies to see which company can give you the deepest discount for multiple mobile/smart phones. There are several of the most up-to-date offers on www.guidetowinningelections.com. Consider buying "reloadable" phones versus subscribing to a longer term contract. Recent legislation has eliminated the ability to change service providers unless you have "purchased" the phone up front.

The candidate, campaign chairman, and campaign coordinators will need phones that can be synced re: schedules and caller lists and anything else they decide needs to be stored precisely on sharing phones. Determine who else on the campaign staff needs a smart phone before you purchase them.

If you have staff members who will often be "on the road" you will want them provided with a phone as well, although it doesn't have to have all the "bells and whistles" provide for the candidate and his key staff.

Because communication among staff and volunteers is critical to the success of any campaign, this is not a place to skimp. You will want your phones to be able to interface with Social Media as well as with each other to keep the word out throughout the day EVERY day of the campaign.

Be sure you have coverage in all areas of your political district before you decide who your provider will be.

Segment your phones into categories such as everyone, volunteers, campaign workers, etc. and stay up to date through events, coordinate schedules, and more via mobile phones.

See more about this in the chapter on Social Media.

EQUIPMENT

One great thing about a campaign is that many people will donate office equipment. You can borrow from individuals, office supply companies, local businessmen or community groups who support your candidate. They will often be able to find some desks, computers, printers, tables and chairs that you can use in the headquarters. (Many volunteers have laptop or tablet computers as well as unlimited calling/texting on cell phones and can bring them to work with when they come to the headquarters to volunteer). Just remember to mark each borrowed item clearly with the name of the owner so the items can be returned promptly when the campaign is over. Keep a complete inventory for insurance purposes as well as for your own use. (It is a good guideline to remember what everyone has loaned when you start writing "thank you" letters).

Depending on the size of the headquarters, the number of staff, and the number of volunteers who come in on a regular basis you will need the following (the amounts are arbitrary—you will have to make your own revisions up or downwards):

- desks with chairs 7 - 8
- large tables with flat surfaces 5 - 7
- folding chairs 20 - 40
- furniture for reception area: 3 - 4 nice chairs coffee table, lamps, etc.
- shelving for supplies and campaign material
- copier/scanner or a 3-in-1 (copier/printer/scanner)
- computers—at least 3 or 4 (but as many as possible)
- WiFi (wireless interface) for electronic equipment
- filing cabinets (one that can be locked)
- clothes rack or clothes tree
- wastepaper baskets and trash cans
- coffee urn and an old refrigerator or soft drink machine
- microwave oven

SUPPLIES

- scratch pads and memo pads
- stationery and envelopes
- file folders and file cards
- copy/printer paper
- paper clips and rubber bands
- mailing labels
- contribution pledge cards
- postage stamps/postage meter/or postage software
- paper towels and toilet paper
- scissors
- large map of district showing precinct boundaries
- pens and pencils
- large manila envelopes
- staplers and staples
- volunteer cards
- campaign literature and materials
- thumb tacks and scotch tape
- hammer, nails, etc.

STAFFING

You should plan to keep your campaign headquarters open six days a week, Monday through Saturday, during the working hours—9 a.m. to 5 p.m. When you get into the heart of the campaign you will want to keep it open during the evening hours also.

The number one rule of a campaign headquarters is that there should always be one person in charge. If the headquarters chairman cannot be present every day, a "day chairman" should be appointed—someone who knows how to work with other people and get things done. Be sure that person has been fully briefed on all details and duties and any business or special events that have been planned for that day.

Most of the work in the headquarters is done by volunteers so try to give them as much advance notice as you can. If you know that a mailing is to be done on Thursday, contact your volunteers on Monday, etc. Remember that these men and women are donating something very precious—their time. (Please do not waste it. Keep them busy. An unhappy volunteer is one who took her time to work in your headquarters and was given nothing to do). That volunteer will probably not come again and may encourage others to stay home as well.

A good rule when working with volunteers is this: have their materials ready for them when they arrive and enough work organized to keep them busy until they leave. Recognize each one by name and thank them when they leave. Volunteers are the lifeblood of your campaign. Treat them that way.

You will also need a good secretary, paid if necessary, to be there on a daily basis. She should be able to do word processing and spreadsheets and work well with people. She will need to be available to the candidate, campaign chairman, public relations person, the headquarters chairman and others. She can train volunteers to help her but she must be in charge of all secretarial functions.

In essence, the activities of the campaign headquarters depend on the headquarters chairman, the volunteers chairman and the secretary working together, setting a positive climate and getting the job done on a daily basis in behalf of the candidate.

COMMUNICATION

Everyone that is working at the headquarters is there for one reason —to get the candidate elected. They are interested and they are concerned. So they should know what is going on. Communications are critical to those working with you.

A bulletin board in the headquarters is invaluable. It should include:

- schedule for the coming week
- news clippings about the candidate
- schedule of the candidate's radio and television
- notices and notes on rallies, parades, barbecues, etc.
- general information of interest to campaign personnel
- announcements of any new staff assignments or committee assignments
- periodic thank yous or encouraging notes from the candidate to volunteers. Even though many of these can be handled by email, it's

always nice to see your name on a bulletin board where everyone can see it.

Have some creative person keep the bulletin board up-to-date and fresh. Change it frequently so everyone will notice it. Take pictures of volunteers working and put them on the board (someone in the campaign will have a color printer—either ink or laser—and pictures can be posted almost immediately after they are taken). Someone may have a digital frame available that you can load and have fresh, rotating pictures for everyone to enjoy.

In this digital age you may also want a volunteer section on the website that has a photo gallery and news items that would be specifically for the cadre of volunteers and headquarters staff.

But, even and maybe especially, in this digital age you need to thank your workers and praise them for a job well done. Have the candidate come through the workroom periodically to give them a pat on the back and some personal thanks. NEVER operate on the philosophy that "If I don't *correct* them, they should know they are doing a good job!" Everyone thrives on positive feedback—especially volunteers. *Be sure they get it.*

7 THE CAMPAIGN TIMETABLE

The person in charge of scheduling for Amtrak knows that in his job, timing is of critical importance. If schedules get out of balance, the result can be a disastrous collision between two trains. In political campaigns, timing is also of immeasurable importance. Along with organizing the precincts, planning and timing rank at the level of highest priority. Without planning, your timing will be off. Without timing, all your planning may result in disappointment on election day. So make your campaign motto. "Let's do the right thing at the right time."

Let's take a look at a very detailed, step-by-step campaign timetable to give you some idea how to set up your own. You may not need anything quite so detailed. You may need to spend more or less time in certain areas, so simply use this as a guide to establish a calendar to meet the needs of your own campaign. Don't forget to include the Social and Database marketing tactics in the coming chapters.

Basically, there are five periods in a campaign, each having its own distinct projects and schedule, but with many overlapping projects and activities. The duration and intensity of the campaign will determine the time needs of each phase, but generally, they will be as follows:

1. The Early Period. This period begins eight to twelve months before election day. In other words, if you are looking at a May primary this stage of the campaign should begin in May and no later than October of the preceding year. Some of the key activities to be included in this initial phase are the following:

- Hold an organization meeting with the key members of your group in order to fill the positions of campaign chairman and co-chairman, as well as finance, research and scheduling chairman. If possible, assign members to the positions of publicity chairman, precinct coordinator, legal counsel and treasurer. If you are not able to fill all these positions at the first meeting, set a time and date for the next meeting to finalize these appointments.

- Legal counsel prepares a file of campaign laws and makes them available and understandable to the members of the campaign committee.

- Begin some quiet fund-raising to cover the immediate expenses. *Go only to those already in "your camp."*

- Begin to schedule appearances for the unannounced candidate so he can become better known as an individual in the community. Get him to as many functions as you possibly can—neighborhood coffees, meetings of civic and service organizations, political meetings, etc. Set up a system of feedback on the impact of each appearance.

- Begin research operations. If it is possible, hire a professional political research team. Otherwise work through your precinct committeemen and volunteers to determine:

  o A statistical analysis of the district—voting patterns, registration data, occupational representation, minority groups, etc.
  o Background on key issues, opponents record, name identification of your candidate, etc.
  o Hold regular meetings of your campaign committee to review progress and plan the next steps.

2. **Off and Running.** This period covers the four to six months before the candidates official announcement of his candidacy. If you are looking at a May primary, this phase should begin in October of the preceding year. You begin to gain momentum during this period. You will need to accomplish the following:

- Have a review process set up to evaluate the progress of each member of the campaign committee. Meet regularly to check this progress and set new goals.

- Complete statistical analysis and study the results carefully.

- Start the first public opinion poll:

    o   Use your professional polling firm, if possible.
    o   If this must be done by volunteers, they should be recruited and trained.

- Have regional and area precinct leaders start building the precinct organization. (See Chapter 3 on the Precinct)

- Begin the search for and selection of professional campaign management—either an individual or an agency—if funds permit and the scope of the campaign requires it.

- Initiate the drive for campaign contributions.

- Have "official campaign photograph" taken of the candidate.

- Design and complete the basic campaign literature—a good brochure spelling out the candidate's background, experience and stand on the issues as well as several flyers on key issues.

- Design basic campaign graphics—a clear, strong logo or slogan that can be used on every campaign piece—something sharp that becomes identified easily with the candidate. Choose colors, style, etc.

- Identify billboard locations and other sign locations that you will wish to reserve later in the campaign. Find out who rents them or from whom permission will be needed.

- Hire an Information Technology expert who can design the website, perform search engine optimization and plan, initiate and monitor the social media program. This person should have an understanding of the political process, the goals of the campaign, as well as expertise in web design, SEO and social media.

- Continue to have the candidate make as many public appearances as possible. By this time word will have "leaked out" that he or she will be a candidate and more invitations to speak should be coming.

- Locate sites for possible headquarters, get rates for rental or preferably, find someone who will be able to donate space.

- Start finding and recruiting volunteers for the campaign headquarters. Get your headquarters chairman or chairwoman on board and begin finding sharp men and women to fill each position. (See Chapter 6: "The Campaign Headquarters). You cannot wait until the day the headquarters opens to begin your search for people to staff it.

- Begin locating donors of office equipment, furniture, computers, printers, etc. The more donors you can find, the less expense there will be for the headquarters. This will make the finance chairman quite happy and leave you more money to promote the candidate.

- Make plans for the official announcement of your person's candidacy. Secure a place and set a time that will get maximum publicity. Prepare invitations to key people in the community and in political leadership positions, such as presidents of the Republican or Democrat women's groups, precinct committeemen and the district chairman, leading businessmen, heads of professional and occupational groups and anyone else who has shown interest in your candidate. And, of course, you will want to invite the press—radio, newspapers, and television. You want to have an enthusiastic and room-filling crowd to show the media that *your* candidate is off and running with large groups of supporters from every segment of the community at his side.

3. **The "Big Splash"** The "official" campaign begins. This period starts about 90 days before election day. (If this is a Congressional or U.S. Senate Race you may need more time in every period) If you are talking about a May primary, this phase of the campaign begins about February 1. However, some states may require a longer period of time between the announcement and the primary election, so be sure to check your state's election code. The period of "the big splash" covers the first 30 days of this 90 day period before the election. You will want to accomplish the following tasks:

- A press conference is called to announce that your candidate is officially declaring himself a candidate for a specific office

- The candidate files the necessary papers to put himself on the ballot. Some states require a filing fee. Others require that a certain number of signatures be filed to qualify him as a candidate. In yet other states, the candidate is nominated to be the party's candidate at a state party convention. Be sure you know your state's code regarding filing dates and requirements that need to be met in order to file as a candidate. See our website for web addresses of state websites that contain the information you need. www.guidetoswillingelections.com.

- Decorate the headquarters and have a "grand opening." Invite the media and everyone you can think of. Use it as a time to recruit volunteers, distribute literature, solicit funds and have people meet the candidate.

- Hold a kick-off rally for supporters and volunteers. Make each one feel a vital part of the campaign and let them catch the excitement and "honor" of working for your candidate.

- Hold a series of fund-raisers

    o A fifty dollar to one hundred dollar per plate dinner, for large givers.
    o A ten dollar per plate barbeque (with all things donated if possible) for smaller givers.
    o Get out a fund-raising letter.

- Distribute press kit to key media contacts.

- Accelerate candidate's public activities. Make as many public appearances and attend as many "coffees" as possible. Visit the "safe" areas shaking hands and passing out brochures in order to give a show of support and garner volunteers. Begin touring outlying areas and shopping centers (Be. sure you have someone or several persons with digital cameras taking pictures and update the website as soon as possible after every event.)

- Work the precincts hard. Register as many voters for your party as possible and have precinct workers identify the preferences of each person registered with your political party.

- Have candidate making as many speeches as possible stressing key issues NOTE: he must stress issues rather than the person who is his opponent in a competitive primary. You do NOT want to make enemies within your own political party. There is no time to "mend fences" between the primary and general election.

- Distribute bumper stickers at every major function. Have someone in shopping center parking lots, etc., who will put them on each car as *owner's permission is obtained.* Have a "bumper sticker blitz."

- Get as many news releases and announcements in the media and on the Internet as possible. Announce appointments of chairmen one by one. Announce formation of special committees and early endorsements. Write news releases regarding the candidate's stand on major issues. The more good announcements and releases you submit the more you will see printed/posted.

- Prepare television and radio "spots" and schedule your time with the stations you wish to use.

- Prepare ads for the Internet and get them placed on as many high ranking sites as possible. Prepare some videos for YouTube. This could simply be someone videotaping one of your candidate's speeches and uploading it. IMPORTANT: the more professional the job, the more points it gets with the voter.

- Obtain endorsements for newspaper ads and prepare the copy. These endorsements are placed on the campaign website as well.

- Secure facilities, equipment, furniture supplies and volunteers for headquarters in outlying areas if such are necessary.

- Begin your second public opinion survey

The "Strong Push." This period covers the second 30 days of the 90 day period preceding the primary election. This phase starts on about March 1. Everyone should be in "full gear" by now. You will need to accomplish the following tasks:

- Begin 25% of the television and radio "spot" schedule. Place small ads in the newspapers.

- Open headquarters in other areas of the district if needed. Schedule each opening in a manner that gets maximum publicity for your candidate.

- Have the candidate make at least one major speech a week dealing with a key issue. Get press releases to the media and see that they get advance texts. Be sure each speech is well attended even if you have to recruit volunteers to enlarge the audience. See to it that someone from your organization is present to hear firsthand what the candidate says (in the event that he may be misquoted in the media) and to give the organization feedback about the audience response. If possible, have someone with a digital video camera record it so it can be featured on the campaign's website. and You Tube.

- Send out your first direct mail piece to all eligible primary voters, giving them reasons why your candidate should get their vote. This can go via snail mail and by e-mail or both.

- Analyze results of second public opinion survey. Adjust speeches and news releases to reflect findings of this poll. NOTE: The candidate cannot change his stand on key issues at this point; however he can soften or strengthen his statements according to poll findings. Revise or remake television and radio "spots" if the poll indicates this is necessary.

- Strengthen any weak spots in the precinct organization.

- Keep sending press releases to the media and online regarding committee appointments, key endorsements and new special committees.

- Begin organizing the "get out the vote" team for election day and start recruiting these volunteers who only help in the "victory squad."

- Put up first wave of billboards in major locations

- Put out a newsletter to all volunteers and other campaign workers, contributors, etc., informing them of the progress of the campaign. You must keep your workers motivated and excited about the campaign.

- Continue the telephone canvassing to identify those voters who are positive toward your candidate as well as those who are undecided.

The Final Days. Now we are really beginning the countdown. All the stops are out during these last 30 days. In a May primary this phase would begin sometime around April 15. Now you MUST accomplish the following tasks:

- Start your full ad schedule on radio and television.

- If the budget permits, saturate the market with ads for your candidate.

- Put up the second wave of billboards. Try to hit all major traffic areas.

- Step up the telephone campaign. Be sure all "doubtfuls" learn more about your candidate through telephone or door-to-door visit.

- Blitz the district with yard signs

- Hold fund-raisers (probably the ten-twenty dollar type)

- Candidate continues to make major speeches, coming down hard on the issues and on the opponent's record if he has one.

- Candidate zeroes in on marginal precincts, going door-to-door in some areas if possible. Volunteers can go door-to-door in these area saying _____, the candidate for _____, asked me to stop by."

- Hold final rally for precinct workers and other volunteers and supporters. Make it exciting, patriotic, etc. and get them "stirred up" for your candidate. They need this for the final "push."

- Precinct workers begin final canvass, handing out literature and checking for those favorable to your candidate who need absentee ballots or assistance on election day.

- Finish recruiting, training and assigning victory squads.

- Brief lawyers task force to assist poll watchers.

- Hold a final press conference for the candidate. Find some key issue or concern that will assure media coverage.

- In the final days, run large (half or full page, if possible) ads in the newspapers. Make the candidate's stand on the issues clear and use large scale listing endorsements.

- Write "thank you" letters to each contributor (if this has not already been done) and to each volunteer and paid worker in the campaign.

- Prepare to deploy all of your database driven Get Out the Friendly Vote strategies—email, robocalls, text message marketing, social media, etc.

The "final days" are at a close. Tomorrow is the big day! Now you need to learn the way to "get out the vote" on election day! For the most exciting day of the campaign go to the next chapter.

8 ELECTION DAY

Everything you have done for the last eight to fourteen months has led to today—ELECTION DAY. Today is the day of truth. Either you win or you lose. But there are still many things you can do to assure a victory because today you "get out the vote."

Remember the chapter on the precinct? Remember that "elections are won or lost in the precinct"? Now you will see firsthand just what that means, because most of our focus on election day is on the precinct. The organization and canvassing you have done in the precinct in the past month will now show up in victory for your candidate if you did it right.

On election day the central campaign headquarters becomes a clearing house—a resource for those of you in the precincts. You call central headquarters to help you, supplying more volunteers, supplies, know-how, etc. They are the clearing house—YOU ARE THE POWERHOUSE! Let us look at what you need and how you function on this big day.

THE PRECINCT HEADQUARTERS

On election day, each precinct should have a headquarters—usually a family house preferably not too far from the polling place. In this headquarters you will need a large room (a garage, a dining room etc) and the following equipment:

- A large precinct map of YOUR precinct

- Work tables and chairs—bridge tables will do nicely

- A spreadsheet of all those voters in your precinct who have made definite commitments to vote for your candidate that you workers have marked with indications of voter's responses to your candidate. Mark "+" for those who are definitely committed to your candidate; mark "-" for those who are *definitely not committed* to your candidate and mark "?" for those who are undecided.

- A spreadsheet of all the voters in your precinct that can be used to check off those who have already voted.

- An "Election Day Kit" for each area in your precinct—perhaps one city block, a certain number of houses, an apartment building, etc.

- Pencils, scratch pads, rubber bands, paperclips, and a steady supply of fresh, hot coffee or ice cold tea.

GETTING ORGANIZED FOR ELECTION DAY

The action really begins the day or two before the election, if your election day effort is to be successful. Believe me, with election day only one day away, your workers will be eager to begin. You will need to call an early morning meeting for the purpose of briefing all your workers and getting your precinct headquarters organized. You want each person to know exactly what to do and how to handle any situation; therefore you will want to call the following people together: the telephoners (one telephoner can call between 50 and 100 people/households, so the number depends on how many people you will need to call), precinct headquarters staff (the precinct captain and two others) the poll watcher, the poll checker, messengers, drivers and baby sitters.

Telephoners

These are the most important people on your team and you need to let them know how much their job is appreciated—they are the ones who turn out the vote. The action for the telephoners begins the day before the election and continues until the polls close, so be sure you have enough volunteers on board and make certain they are properly trained. The day before the election you should have a worker assigned to call every voter identified as a positive vote for your candidate. You want to remind them that the next day is election day and that the candidate is counting on their vote. This has a great impact on the voters called, making them feel important and needed. AND it certainly increases the likelihood that they will, indeed, get to the polls and vote for your candidate.

You will want to give each of your telephoners a list of names and phone numbers of those friendly voters to be called—one person can handle from fifty to one hundred calls in a day—if you can recruit enough volunteers to insure that no one has more than fifty names you can do a terrific job! Give each telephoner a sample message, a message that is friendly, brief and to the point. This makes it easier for those who are more timid or have no imagination and it also eliminates many mistakes. The following is a sample message you can adapt to your own precinct and candidate:

> Hello. My name is _____, Jim Green, our candidate for the State Senate, asked me to call you to remind you that tomorrow is election day and to tell you he is counting on your vote. The polling place for our precinct is Edison School on the corner of 16th Street and Elm and the polls will be open from 6 a.m. until 7 p.m. Remember, be sure to vote for Jim Green for state senate. Goodbye."

This brief message takes only a moment but gleans terrific results. It is helpful, too, if you have inexperienced telephoners go through a few "practice" calls during the briefing session to help them get the feel of handling the calls when questions are asked or comments made. The old saying, "practice makes perfect" certainly applies when you are training people to use the telephone in a campaign.

The second phase of the telephoner's job begins in the early afternoon on election day. Have them report to the precinct headquarters at approximately 1 p.m. to pick up the lists of those who have not yet voted (the poll checker will have obtained from the precinct voting place the list of those who have voted and the headquarters staff will then make a list of the friendly (+) voters to be called and reminded that they have not voted) You might want to give them a message such as this:

> Hello. My name is _____, and I am calling you from Jim Green's headquarters. Our records indicate that you have not had the opportunity of voting. I wonder if you need a ride to the polls or a babysitter to make it possible for you to get away long enough to vote? Jim Green certainly would appreciate your vote for state senator. Can he count on your getting to the polling place before it closes? Thank you. Goodbye.

If the voter indicates that he or she needs a ride to the polls or a babysitter, get that information to your precinct headquarters immediately. If after you have called several times and receive no answer, you need to report this to headquarters so a doorknob hanger can be left at their home, an e-mail sent or some other follow-up arranged.

Precinct Headquarters Staff

The precinct captain and two volunteers to work as clerical help should be able to handle the precinct headquarters. But in selecting your staff, be sure you find volunteers who keep calm under pressure—things can get hectic at times and you do not need someone who gets snappy on the phone or cries easily when things get a bit too busy. Their basic job will be to compile the lists of those "friendlies" who have not voted. Have the telephoners come by the precinct headquarters about 2:30 p.m. and pick up those names. The telephoners should directly contact your drivers or precinct headquarters to drive voters to the polls or do babysitting if the need arises. A few competent teenagers can be helpful in the afternoon when doorknob hangers need to be left on the doors of those not contacted by phone.

Poll Watcher

This person's job is to be sure that no illegal voting or election fraud takes place at the polls. Get a strong person, if possible—one who cannot be intimidated. It is still an all too frequent occurrence that someone will try to vote for a registered voter who has moved or died, but not been taken off the rolls. If you have done your "homework" in the preceding months, you will have identified every eligible and registered voter in your precinct. You will then have no surprises on election day that you cannot handle.

The poll watcher should plan to be "on duty" from the time the polls open until the last ballot is cast. He should bring with him a letter of authorization stating that he is the official poll watcher for the candidate or the party in this precinct. In addition he needs to bring the names of the non-eligible voters, kept on a spreadsheet in alphabetical order for easy access. The reason why they are not eligible should be included; e.g., they have moved, are deceased, no such address, etc. (This information has been obtained by precinct workers who keep up-to-date on every residence in their assigned area. They keep track of every change in voters that takes place and are able to verify these changes on the spreadsheet). The candidate or party organization also may find ineligible voters by sending out a mailing a few weeks before election day and marking the envelop "Do Not Forward, Return to Sender." The returned mailings will be marked by the Postal Service as "Not at This Address," "Deceased", "Moved", "No such address," etc. This returned envelope is valuable proof that the person standing in line is probably not eligible to vote.

The poll watcher should also have a copy of the election code page pertaining to the provisions for and the rights of poll watchers. Because of his "delicate" position, he needs to know exactly what is legally allowed.
As soon as the poll watcher arrives at the polling place he should, after introducing himself, begin to study the list of voters and compare it with his list, looking for any ineligible names. If anyone does come to vote when they are not eligible, the poll watcher should step forward immediately and say to the election board official, "Pardon me, but I challenge that voter." Then he should state the basis for the challenge!

When asked for identification or proof of residency, the challenged voter will either try to make a quick exit or try to bluff his or her way through. If the election official waives the challenge, hoping to keep the line moving, the poll watcher should request the election official to call the County Clerk for advice or assistance. He should inform the election official that he will file a formal charge of fraud with the county prosecutor if this challenged voter is not properly checked.

It is important that the poll watcher remain calm, courteous and firm. He is well within the law as long as his own conduct is proper. He must keep in mind that he is preventing an illegal vote. If one vote is so precious that the opposition will try a fraud to get it, then it is important enough for your side to work to prevent that illegal vote. Remember that elections are sometimes won or lost by less than one vote per precinct.

Poll Checker

It is the poll checker's job to be at the polls to check the lists when they are available, to see who has voted and who has not. As he goes down his list of voters, he checks off those who have voted and gets the information back to the precinct headquarters usually around Noon, and then later about 4 PM . He will have a spreadsheet with the name of every voter in the precinct who has a "+" for your candidate. He may have a "tear sheet"—a copy of the voter list used by the election board and provided for the checkers of each political party. If this is the case, he simply obtains his copy of the "tear sheet" and gets it to the precinct headquarters. Whatever the system in your district, be sure you know it and have devised an efficient plan to get the names of those who have voted to the precinct headquarters at regular intervals.

As the voting comes near the end and there are crowds of voters waiting in line, the poll checker may want to stand near enough to the election board tables to hear the names as they are called. He then can check them off and get these names to the headquarters so an accurate count can be made and last minute calls can be placed.

The poll checker should, by all means, be courteous. He should have with him a copy of the election code section that may pertain to poll checkers and, if challenged, be able to defend his presence according to the code.

Messengers, Drivers and Babysitters

These people do exactly what their titles imply; i.e., the messengers act as "runners" between the precinct headquarters and the polling place or wherever the captain needs them to go. Teens who are able to drive are superb in this position. Housewives with station wagons and/or vans and young children at home or in daycare are usually quite willing to drive those voters who have no transportation to the polls and wait for them while they vote. Most of them will be willing to stop by and babysit while a mother with small children goes to vote. Mothers with small children will often offer their babysitting services to those women who can bring their children to the babysitter's home on their way to the polls and pick them up after they have cast their ballot. Do not be afraid to be creative when it comes to thinking of ways to get people to the polls. Remember—EVERY VOTE COUNTS!

After the Polls Close

Even though you may be tired after a long day of "turning out the vote," you will not want to go home and rest. Hopefully, now is the time to celebrate as you watch those election returns come it. At least have a precinct celebration for all your workers—some cold drinks and "munchies" and lots of "thank yous." If you create a spirit of teamwork and make each person feel that he or she was a vital part of that team, they will be eager to help in the next campaign.

CENTRAL HEADQUARTERS

While most of the action is in the precinct, there are still things to be done at central headquarters. Basically the central headquarters is in charge of the "victory squad"—special election day forces made up of those people who could not or would not get involved in the campaign on a long term basis but want to work on election day. They are used to cover your weak precincts and help "get out the vote." The precinct captains let central headquarters know where their weak spots are and someone from "the victory squad" can be assigned to go there on election day. They may be used in telephoning, as a messenger, checker, etc., or even on the election board.

The regular staff of the central headquarters will not have time to wonder what their functions are that day. They will be busy answering the phones, meeting with the press, fending off worry-warts who "drop by" but will not do anything constructive other than wanting to "advise" the precinct captain and dealing with emergencies. They will be "tying up the loose ends" and already planning for the general election.

THE GENERAL ELECTION

The returns are in, your candidate has won! You take time to celebrate, but even during the celebration you are planning the final phase of the campaign leading up to the general election.

The general election is run very much like the primary election with a few exceptions:

In the primary election you were dealing only with registered voters of your political party. In the general election you are dealing with ALL registered voters and so you must, again, identify those who are for, against, or undecided about your candidate. You have to retain the positives, persuade the undecideds and hope that the negatives forget the election is around the corner. Now your precinct organization is more important than ever and must be orchestrated like a great symphony. You do the same thing you did in the primary, only better and on a wider scale. You will want to incorporate as many of your primary opponent's workers into your campaign as possible and unify the party so you have as much strength as you can get.

You do not want to have any regrets or enemies in your own party during the campaign for the general election. You want to spend time defeating your opponent, not building bridges to estranged fellow party workers.

In the primary election you had from eight to fourteen months leading up to election day. In the general election you may have six months at the most and in some states only three months, to convince the voters that your candidate is the person for the job.

Your fund raising base will be broader now, but you have less time in which to gather funds. The more your candidate has the look of the "winner," the easier it will be to obtain significant contributions.

Voter registration may be resumed. Find as many unregistered voters as you can who will probably be for your candidate and get them registered.

Never forget the importance of the precinct. Whether it is a school board race or a state wide race for governor or United States Senate, the votes are still cast in the precinct. If you ignore the precinct and rely totally on the media, you may consider your race lost before election day arrives. If you work those precincts, getting every possible vote for your candidate, you can win on a small budget. The key to success in elections—in the primary or the general—is the precinct.

The "secret" the pros have never told you—is the secret of the precinct.

9 TRADITIONAL COMMUNICATIONS & P.R.

The team was going to the state championship playoffs! It was an honor well deserved because the members had trained hard, played fair and clean and each one had done his part to make it a successful team effort. The coach was ecstatic! The championship could mean his big break—an open door to the pros. And he had a plan—a wonderful new play that should mean certain victory. With great excitement and assurance he approached the big game knowing that there was no way his team could lose. BUT THEY WERE DEFEATED! Why? Because he had failed to share his wonderful and infallible play with his team. He had failed to communicate.

A political campaign is also a team fighting the opposition for the championship—victory at the polls. And no matter how wonderful the campaign strategy, no matter how great the candidate, no matter how clear the issues—unless the workers know the plan and the voters are convinced to vote for you candidate, you will lose. It is as simple as that.

This business of communication and public relations is vital to the success of any winning campaign. We need to take a close look at it. A review of Wikipedia's description of the terms "communication" and public relations" helps you see their significance.

COMMUNICATION is the activity of conveying meaningful information. Communication requires a sender, a message, and an intended recipient, although the receiver need not be present or aware of the sender's intent to communicate at the time of communication; thus communication can occur across vast distances in time and space. Communication requires that the communicating parties share an area of communicative commonality. The communication process is complete once the receiver *has understood* the message of the sender.

PUBLIC RELATIONS, abbreviated as **PR**, is the actions of a corporation, store, government, individual, etc., in promoting goodwill between itself and the public, the community, employees, customers, etc. Public relations is used to build rapport with employees, customers, investors, voters, or the general public. Almost any organization that has a stake in how it is portrayed in the public arena employs some level of public relations.

There we have it. Communications is delivering the message and public relations is winning the public approval—two critically essential tasks in any political campaign. We are going to combine the two and consider them together as one function. In a small campaign, a committee or individual may be able to handle all public relations functions; however, in a larger race—for governor or the U.S. Congress or Senate—you will need a professional public relations person or firm to handle the extensive and complex interfacing with the public and the media.

Basically, there are four ways a candidate communicates with the public: through

- graphics

- direct mail

- personal appearance

- the use of the media which includes digital media—the website, social media, video, etc.

It is not enough to choose *one* of these avenues of communication. Rather, in a winning campaign, each is used to the best advantage to give the greatest and the most positive exposure of the candidate to the voters. A plan is drawn up based on information gleaned from the surveys, using each method to its ultimate potential. Let us take a closer look at each of these ways of reaching and convincing voters that your candidate is THE ONE.

GRAPHICS

Graphics is the term used to refer to all the material prepared for the campaign team and used to "sell" the candidate to the public. The "star of the graphics show" is the website and use of social media but it also includes brochures, buttons, bumper stickers, yard signs, billboards and "gimmicks" such as shopping bags, litterbags, balloons, etc. They are used mainly to give a quick sketch of the candidate and to build name identification. The more people see the name, the more likely they are to recognize it and respond to it positively in the voting booth. A few rules in the use of graphics include:

- *Plan.* Determine ahead of time what your budget will allow, know how much name identification you need to build and just what the voters in your district will respond to best.

- *Design.* Find a professional who knows the basics of good design, the use of color and has a way with words. Develop your graphics around a central theme to multiply the impact and keep it simple. You are not trying to win the Nobel prize in literature—you are trying to gain votes. Use high quality material to show you have a high quality candidate. *Be consistent, don't keep changing the "look and feel" of the campaign.*

- *Originality.* Campaign material can be deadly dull unless some originality and creativity are used. Make your literature stand out from the "run of the mill" graphics. Gather all the campaign material of other candidates that you can find. Analyze it and make yours better!

- *Distribute.* Plan for the most efficient and effective distribution possible.

  o Hand out brochures, buttons, bumper stickers at rallies and other functions involving large numbers of people. Go door-to-door.

  o Secure billboard locations very early in the campaign to insure the best locations and the most beneficial periods of time.

  o Get permission to place yard signs early so that at the peak of the campaign you can have a yard sign "blitz"—suddenly your candidate's name appears everywhere and it seems that every household or neighborhood is endorsing your candidate.

DIRECT MAIL

Direct mail can be used as one of the most effective tools in the campaign, if it is used correctly. The primary function of direct mail is to focus on a specific group with a message tailored to their specific interests. For example, a mailing can be sent to members of the Gun Owner's Association or Rifle Association, if gun control is an issue in the campaign and your candidate opposes it. If your candidate is strong on traditional family issues he will certainly want to send a mailing to all members of each "pro-family" group in his district. The possibilities are endless. And not only can he garner votes from these groups, but he can recruit volunteers and ask for campaign contributions at the same time.

Of course the issue selected would depend on whether the desired seat is on a local, state or federal level. You would not, for example, send a mailing about federal taxes if you are running for a state house seat. Nor would you feature a local tax if you are running for the U.S. Senate.

As the cost of direct mail continues to escalate, it is even more important to plan carefully what you intend to do with it. A combination of good timing, content and targeting can provide the formula that will make a particular mailing the force that tips the election scales in your favor.

Some things you need to keep in mind when using direct mail are:

- Make it clear why the reader should vote for your candidate. State logically and clearly the benefits and advantages of your candidate's beliefs and stands on the issues over his opponents.

- Be sincere and forthright. Do not exaggerate or use forced humility or other insincerities that may irritate the reader. Do not talk down to your reader.

- Keep your mailing neat and clean. Do not wait until the last minute to get the mailing ready and then have to accept smudges, crooked stamps and grammatical errors. There is no excuse for sloppiness in direct mail. A sloppy letter creates the image of a sloppy candidate in the mind of the reader.

- Personalize the letter as much as possible. In this day of word processors, it is possible to repeat the reader's name in the content of the letter. You can also personalize it by having your workers pen notes on the letter calling the reader's attention to a particular issue. The more personal it is, the better it will be received.

- Plan the mailing to be delivered at the right time in the campaign. For example, you may want to call attention to a particular television program about your candidate or point out the date of a large rally at the same time you are informing the reader about your candidate. Or you may plan for the letter to arrive the day before election day to give the reader one last bit of information about your candidate and reinforce the name recognition. You must know how long it takes a mailing to be delivered in your town. A mailing that arrives the day after the election is a waste of time, material and money and serves no purpose whatever.

The successful candidate knows that the best mailing is often the simplest—a postcard, reaching voters at precisely the right moment can often be the factor that wins that last vote needed to carry each precinct.

PERSONAL APPEARANCES

Nothing has quite the impact as a personal appearance on the part of the candidate. When and where he appears must be determined by his speaking abilities and his personal appearance. Assuming that he has all the attributes of a good candidate and is a credible speaker, you can utilize these talents. Some of the opportunities for personal appearance are door-to-door visits; small gatherings such as coffees, desserts, etc., and large gatherings such as rallies, debates and speeches to specific groups.

Door to Door Visits

A threshold visit is a convincing way for a candidate to present himself as one interested in the problems and concerns of his constituents. In small campaigns it is possible to visit every family in the district as long as he keeps his presentation brief and makes good use of his time. In 1980 David O'Hara won a seat in the state legislature of Montana, unseating the Speaker of the House. His secret? He went to every house in his legislative district and he won by an overwhelming margin.

If the candidate himself cannot knock on every door, he can recruit volunteers who will visit each house in his behalf. A simple greeting such as, "Hello I am Mable Brown. Jim Green, a candidate for mayor, asked me to visit you and give you this literature about him and his stand on the issues. Can he count on your vote?"The fact that you took your time on behalf of the candidate to visit every home on the block gives a positive message to the person answering the door and the literature you leave will restate the message. Some points to keep in mind are:

- Be sure your appearance is one that speaks well of the candidate. Clean clothes and combed hair are just two of the essential points of good grooming. A pleasant manner and smile may say as much or more than your words.

- Keep your message brief and simple. Above all, NEVER get into an argument with the person answering the door. If he is adamantly opposed to your candidate, thank him graciously for his time and leave. Do *not* go in. You can accomplish your task at the door in a few minutes and move on to the next house. Have some knowledge of such facts as: a) how they can register to vote; b) when absentee voting begins and ends and how to obtain an absentee ballot; c) who they can contact if they wish to volunteer in the campaign; and d) where they go to vote.

Small Groups

Small groups can be almost as effective as a threshold visit because it gives each person an opportunity to meet and visit with the candidate. You can arrange a coffee or dessert for friends and neighbors. This is most effective in a small race or early in a large race for the recruitment of volunteers. Keep in mind that your candidate can only stretch so far. Do not use up all his energy going to small functions late in the campaign.

Rallies and Speeches

Rallies and speeches generally involve larger crowds enabling your candidate to reach more people at one time. If he is a good speaker, this can definitely be used to his advantage and the more large gatherings you can program into his schedule, the more headway you can make in the campaign.

A rally is generally a gathering of people for the particular purpose of seeing and hearing a candidate. It is also a way to show public support for his candidacy and possibly attract the media for new coverage. It should have an atmosphere of excitement about the candidate and an attitude of victory.

A rally can be promoted for your candidate only, or for all the candidates in your political party who are running for the various offices. If it is for your candidate alone, he has a chance to shine—to make a major speech and be the center of attraction. He should plan a major statement and prepare it so well that there is no chance for mistakes in his presentation. On the other hand, if he is joining with other candidates there are some certain guidelines he should follow. He should make a punchy, clear presentation, *keeping within the time limit set for him.* A candidate who drones on and on at such a rally is remembered alright, but not positively. The one who delivers a short, clear, dynamic statement is the one who steals the show.

Speech opportunities to various groups are generally readily available if your candidate has any talent for speaking at all. The civic groups in your community are always looking for someone to bring a message. Various interest groups will seek him out. Schedule your candidate for as many of these as time and his energy allow; because it gives him a wide exposure to the community. Be sure he prepares these speeches. Candidates often get themselves "out on a limb" when they try to address a group "off the cuff."

THE NON-DIGITAL MEDIA

The "Media" includes newspapers, radio and television—each of which reaches a large number of people with their message. The use of social media will be discussed in the Chapter 15. It is possible to win a campaign without the support of the media, but having them on your side or at least neutral can be a great assist. There are basically six tools to use in communicating through the media: 1) letters to the editor; 2) endorsements and news releases; 3) press conferences; 4) "one-on-one" interviews; 5) news stories, and 6) paid political announcements, advertisements and "spots."

Letters to the Editor

This has traditionally been one of the best ways of getting free publicity for your candidate and his views on a continuing basis. It still can be used to your candidate's advantage. Most "average" readers interpret one letter to the editor as a representative of many others who hold the same opinion. Therefore, letters to the editor can be an important part of the campaign, especially during the last two months of a campaign when issues are clearly defined. Some guidelines for writing letters to the editor are:

- A letter should be sent by a different supporter of your candidate every day throughout the campaign. The public relations chairman should recruit a group of people who are able to write fairly well and plan "who writes when about what." A letter to the editor campaign does not "just happen"—it has to be orchestrated.

- Concentrate on *selected issues* and subjects. Choose only those issues that have wide support among the voters in your constituency.

- Be sure the letters are well written, easily understood and address one issue only. *Never use the same letter twice.*

- Support your candidate in the letter. Spell his name correctly and mention it more than once if possible.

- Keep the letter brief.

Remember that not every letter will be printed, but if you and your candidate's supporters write enough letters, the paper will find it impossible to ignore them all. Just hang in there and "keep those cards and letters going!"

Endorsements and News Releases

Normally one of the first things we do when we see a list of names of people who are for or against a candidate or a program is to glance through it to see which names we recognize. Endorsements carry a great deal of clout and it is important that you get endorsements from as many people as you can. It is helpful to get endorsements from groups such as the Policemen's Association, Homeowner's Association, Senior Citizen groups, Anti-Pornography groups, etc. The more groups, associations and individuals that will endorse your candidate and allow their name to be used on campaign literature and in newspaper advertisements, the stronger you make your candidate appear. You must have their signature giving you permission to use their name; therefore, it is wise throughout the campaign to carry cards that you can have completed at coffees, rallies, gatherings of any kind. If you don't have a website that allows people to sign up, endorse your candidate, volunteer to host an event, etc, a card something like this will be quite helpful:

Name (please print) _____

Address _____

_____

Phone _____

I would like to help in the campaign of Joe Green for Mayor

☐ Work at campaign headquarters   ☐ Do telephoning from home

☐ Write letters to the editor   ☐ Be on a speaker's panel

☐ Help in fund raising   ☐ Hold a coffee in my home

☐ You may use my name in campaign literature, news paper advertisements and other campaign efforts. I heartily endorse the candidacy of Joe Green for Mayor.

Signature _____

When a major group endorses your candidate be sure to announce it in the form of a "news release." If the news release is not printed, have the spokesman for the group write a letter to the editor stating such an endorsement has been given.

A press release, however, is not confined only to announcements of endorsements. It can be used for major statements on issues, the announcement of a key worker in his campaign, the description of a major campaign event, to name a few. The press releases should also be submitted to online PR sites.

In a press release, be sure to give facts only, not opinion, and state them clearly and concisely. Be sure to have a contact person in case the media personnel want to ask for clarification or for further information. Be certain your facts are accurate and that the release is written clearly briefly and without grammatical error.

A sample press release is given on below:

JOE GREEN FOR MAYOR

FOR IMMEDIATE RELEASE
CONTACT: George Smith
PHONE: 123-456-7890

TODAY'S DATE: 3-14-13

SUBJECT: Endorsement of Joe Green by Citizens for Safe Streets

The Citizens for Safe Streets of Ourtown endorses Joe Green for Mayor.

Mary Ann Little of Ourtown's Citizen's for Safe Streets stated, "Joe Green has consistently worked with the Ourtown Police Department to keep our streets safe while he was a member of the city council. He lead the movement to form block watch groups and helped raise funds to increase the number of street lights in our neighborhoods. Further he has worked tirelessly to establish activity centers for children and teens for after school activities. We believe that Joe Green is exactly the kind of mayor we need in Ourtown"

Little stated further, "We are going to put our full effort behind getting Joe Green elected and hope others who are interested in a safer community will join with us in this effort."

Press Conference

The press conference is really a media event. Notices are sent to every newspaper, radio station and television station announcing the time and place of the press conference. A dynamic medium of communication between the candidate and the press, it can be a source of favorable and far-reaching publicity. However, used ineptly, it can result in irreparable damage to a campaign.

There are two types of press conferences and each is handled differently. The first is the press conference held as a result of an emergency—to rebut a smear, to announce an important endorsement by an important public figure, etc. The second type of press conference is to deal with subject matter that is important to a wide variety of people and that cannot be covered by a news release.

Before calling a press conference you must be certain that your facts are straight and complete and that your candidate can handle questions by the press on any aspect of his campaign. The press, with their ability and desire to probe can turn a simple announcement into a disaster for your campaign unless you have done your homework well.

"One-on-One Interview"

Radio and television interviews give the candidate a chance to explain in greater detail what his stands are on the issues and gives the voter the greatest chance to see what the candidate is really like.

Even though you are working with an interviewer who may or may not favor your candidate, it is possible for the candidate to be in control. To be in control he must be prepared, be positive and be sincere. In preparing for the interview, the candidate should know what he wants to stress before going into the interview. He can guide the interview, not by changing the subject or answering questions that were not asked, but by leading the interviewer to areas he wants to cover. When you are discussing problem areas, be positive, offering solutions rather than merely citing problems. The voters want to know what you intend to do to solve them rather than what you think about them. And, finally, state your argument sincerely.

Your sincerity and conviction may be more convincing than your words. (One thought worthy of note, if you are on television try to appear relaxed and use your smile—this gives you the appearance of "having nothing to hide").

When speaking on radio or television, remember that your audience does not know what is in your mind—you must explain clearly what you mean. Do not assume that your audience knows all that you know. Speak slowly enough that they can understand you and NEVER interrupt your interviewer. Keep calm and think before answering. A sense of humor, used wisely can save what could be a disastrous interview.

In addition to terrestrial (land based) radio, consider expanding to Internet talk radio and satellite based shows. Make sure to include links or copies of your radio and television interviews on the website, and promote them via social media.

News Stories

News stories can be planned if you have a creative and industrious public relations person or firm. News stories are free campaign coverage and reach more people than any paid advertising could do. Several years ago a candidate for the U.S. Congress in one of the Western states worked in a different occupation every day for a week. He rode the garbage truck; he pumped gas at the corner filling station; he worked as an orderly in the local hospital; and he drove a tractor on a farm. Every day, the television cameras were cranking away showing him "on the job." It took one week of his time plus some discomfort and embarrassment, but he could never have raised enough money to buy that kind of media coverage. It was a gimmick, but it worked. If you can think of something more exciting than shaking hands and kissing babies, the media will most likely be there.

Paid Political Announcements, Advertisements and "Spots"

In this day of mass media coverage, more and more of the campaign budget is spent "buying :time" for television and radio announcements and for advertising in the local newspaper. It is through these avenues that you reach the persons who are indifferent. You more or less "sneak up on them" when they are watching something else.

Buying time on radio and television stations requires a certain expertise, if you have any budget for it at all. An amateur trying to do such a job can often do more harm than good for the campaign. It is wise to work through a public relations person or firm who has such expertise, or use the services of an advertising agency. The time must be scheduled well in advance, if you are to get the best time slots before your opponent or other candidates schedule it for themselves.

Preparing the brief five or fifteen minute program should also be left to some experts who know how to make your candidate look his best and make the greatest positive impression on the audience. You want your candidate to come across as intelligent, knowledgeable on the issues, compassionate, in touch with the needs of the voters and capable of finding solutions to the problems of his constituents. People with the "know how" can help him project just such an image.

In summary, the purpose of the whole campaign is to communicate to the voters that your candidate is truly the one most qualified for the position and to convince them to cast their vote for him on election day.

10 SHOW ME THE MONEY!

Did you ever go to the grocery store, fill your cart until it bulged and overflowed with food and discovered at the checkout counter than you had forgotten your check book and couldn't find your debit card in your purse or wallet—and you were out of cash? Did they say, "Oh, that's O.K. Take your groceries and enjoy them?" Of course they did not! You left the groceries with the checker and ran home to get your check book and/or debit card or cash. *They got the money before you got the groceries!*

Did you ever write a number of checks for "special" expenditures, especially at Christmas, only to get a notice from the bank that you had overdrawn your account? It seems redundant to state that they probably did not give you a call or add to the bottom of the notice, "Don't worry about it. We know you meant well. Pay us when you can."

Just because you have the lofty ideal of electing a statesman to public office, someone who will save the taxpayers money and will tighten the belt of government spending, it does not mean that his campaign debts will be forgiven. No way! And campaigns are very expensive operations. It is necessary, therefore, that we take a look at budgeting and fundraising— something without which the campaign cannot continue.

BUDGETING

Even in the smallest campaign, budgeting is critical. If you have no idea how much money you need to spend, you don't know how much money you need to raise. Generally, contributions don't just come floating in after you announce your candidacy. They have to be sought out, worked for, solicited. Every penny counts and must be spent wisely. Running a campaign without a budget is like touring the United States without a map or a GPS—you may get where you want to go and then again, you may not.

In preparing a realistic budget, you should list everything in the campaign that incurs an expense from paperclips to salaries. To do this you need to get estimates on major items such as printing, television and radio spots, newspaper ads and major office equipment and supplies. You need to determine how much office furniture and equipment can be donated, whether you can get space donated for the headquarters and whether you can run the headquarters totally with volunteers rather than paid staff. The more donations of time and materials you can obtain through donations, the less money you will need to budget and raise for the total campaign. And you will be able to spend the money you have on those critical purchases of media time.

If you start with a "no frills" budget, you will not have to experience the pain of cutting and cutting to make ends meet. You may still have to do some trimming but it will not be nearly so traumatic. Work with your committees to determine what kind of materials they will need, what quantities they will use and how much they estimate the cost to be. The more input you have, the more realistic the budget will be. The more your key workers are involved, the more they will be able to work within the budget THEY have helped prepare.

The next few pages give you some samples of "work sheets" that will be helpful to setting up your own budget. You need to be able to estimate how much you will need to spend each month for every item and then project what the overall cost will be for the campaign. This is a "work sheet" and will need to be revised periodically as your campaign needs change so be sure to date each draft. This can be done much more easily and effectively on a computer generated spreadsheet.

PRIMARY ELECTION BUDGET WORK SHEET DATE _____

EXPENDITURES	FEB	MAR	APR	MAY	JUNE
RESEARCH & ANALYSIS					
Professional Services					
Polling					
Lists					
Misc. Expenses					

TOTALS BY MONTH					
STAFF					
Salaries					
Taxes					
Expenses					
Travel					
Meals(if any)					
TOTAL BY MONTH					
HEADQUARTERS					
Rent					
Utilities					
Telephone					
Furniture					
Computer equipment, copier, etc.					
Insurance					
Supplies					
Decorations					
TOTALS BY MONTH					
CANDIDATE					
Travel					
Telephones					
Meals and Expenses					
TOTAL BY MONTH					
COMMUNICATIONS AND P.R.					

Personnel salaries or fees					
Direct Mail					
Printing					
Postage					
Radio					
Production					
Time					
Television					
Production					
Time					
Newspaper Ads					
Production					
Space					
Billboards					
Production					
Space Rental					
Web Site & Social Media					
Online Advertising					
Mobile Phone Costs					
TOTALS BY MONTH					
FUND RAISING					
Stationery and Supplies					
Postage					
Travel					

Entertainment					
TOTALS BY MONTH					
CONTINGENCY FUND					
TOTALS BY MONTH					

FUND RAISING

Even before you finish the budget you need to start fundraising. In fact, fund-raising needs to begin the moment your candidate says he will run. One of the key persons of your campaign committee is your finance chairman, and he should be "on board" early and begin to put together his finance committee.

The chairman of the finance committee, as we said in Chapter Five, should be a leader in the community and have sufficient funds to contribute generously to the campaign. He, then, should select other outstanding citizens who represent various key segments of the community, e.g., a leader in the medical and dental field, a leader in the construction industry, a lawyer, a key retailer, and leaders in the industrial and agricultural areas. etc. Each of these members of the committee should, in turn select a handful of people in their own profession or occupation who can help solicit funds from their peers. Once you have your general committee and occupational sub-committees formed, it is time to plan your fund raising activities. Do not be afraid to be creative, to try new and different things to get people to part with their money joyfully in behalf of your candidate. And remember—no contribution is too small. Seek out larger givers, certainly, but do not be afraid to appeal for smaller gifts of five dollars, ten dollars and twenty-five dollars. In this day of the ATM $20 is "king" and should be gladly received and a receipt given with a smile. All of these added up can make a sizeable difference in the "war-chest," and each contributor feels he has an important part in the campaign.

Federal Guidelines

Races for non-federal offices are governed by individual state and local law. Over half the states allow some level of corporate and union contributions. Some states have limits on contributions from individuals that are lower than the national limits, while four states

(Missouri, Oregon, Utah and Virginia) have no limits at all. This article deals primarily with campaigns for federal office.

Once a candidate has declared his candidacy, he is responsible for reporting any contribution of more than two hundred dollars. He must list the name, address and occupation of the donor. Therefore, it is important to keep accurate records of all contributions. Federal statutes stipulate that each person can give up to $2,600 to each candidate in any federal election. But he cannot give more than $32,400 total for the year to federal campaigns. That means that each person can give $2,600 to your candidate in both the primary and the general elections.

Contribution Limits 2013-14

	To each candidate or candidate committee per election	To national party committee per calendar year	To state, district & local party committee per calendar year	To any other political committee per calendar year[1]	Special Limits
Individual may give	$2,600*	$32,400*	$10,000 (combined limit)	$5,000	$123,200* overall biennial limit: • $48,600* to all candidates • $74,600* to all PACs and parties[2]
National Party Committee may give	$5,000	No limit	No limit	$5,000	$45,400* to Senate candidate per campaign[3]
State, District & Local Party Committee may give	$5,000 (combined limit)	No limit	No limit	$5,000	No limit
PAC (multicandidate)[4] may give	$5,000	$15,000	$5,000 (combined limit)	$5,000	No limit
PAC (not multicandidate) may give	$2,600*	$32,400*	$10,000 (combined limit)	$5,000	No limit
Authorized Campaign Committee may give	$2,000[5]	No limit	No limit	$5,000	No limit

Source: http://www.fec.gov/pages/brochures/fecfeca.shtml#Contribution_Limits

Each member of his family can also contribute $2,600 for each election. The FEC considers primaries, general and runoff elections as SEPARATE elections.

For more detailed information about federal and state guidelines, have your finance chairman or legal counsel contact the Federal Elections Commission, the Secretary of State in your state and the state headquarters of your political party. Once you know how to handle the reports and records, get busy! Let us take a look at some of the ways you can bring some contributions now into the campaign treasury.

(For links to specific websites in your state go to our site at:

http://www.guidetowinningelections.com/).

Major Dinners

This is one of the most common and successful ways to raise campaign funds, but there are many different approaches to giving a "campaign dinner." We will look at some of them, but they are limited only by your imagination.

First, there is the *Testimonial Dinner*—a time to pay tribute to a great man (your candidate) and "kick off" his campaign. This can be especially successful if your candidate is an incumbent (Perhaps he is a state legislator who is running for the office of governor or U.S. Congress). Find yourself a well known "personality" to act as a "draw," one preferably who does not expect a generous honorarium, and begin planning. Do not be afraid to charge a large sum, say one hundred to two hundred dollars per person (or more), and invite the leading business and professional men and women in the community. Make it a "high class" affair, one at which people will want to be seen. At the affair have a number of leading citizens praise your candidate for his "service to the community," and then ask those attending to fill out a card pledging to raise "X" amount of dollars for the campaign over the next two months. Be sure to have someone who is dynamic and not afraid to ask for money. Help the audience feel that it is a great privilege and to their benefit to donate to this campaign.

Specialty fund-raising dinners such as spaghetti dinners, barbeques, pot-lucks and luaus can be used with different groups with differing economic abilities. If you believe a major dinner is more than you can handle, have something less demanding such as a watermelon bust in the summer or an ice cream social. Have a pizza party for the young people and enlist them as volunteers—this can be as important as money in some instances.

Luncheons are in the same category as dinners. Have the different occupational representatives on your finance committee plan a luncheon for your candidate, inviting the leaders in his profession or occupation. Have your candidate address the group, paying particular attention to their needs and concerns and giving them time for questions and answers. If your candidate is enthusiastic and interested in them, as well as concerned for their issues, they will respond generously when asked for contributions and volunteers. And they will not be hesitant in recommending your candidate to other members of their group.

Direct Mail

In planning your direct mail fund-raising outreach you will need to consider both the personal letter and the mass mailing if you are to use mailings to their maximum.

The personal letter can be used by the candidate as well as the members of his campaign committee and, especially, his finance committee. Each letter can be personalized as to approach. For example, members of the campaign committee can emphasize just why the candidate is so outstanding that they would be spending their time and energy trying to help him get elected—he is, for example, hard working, honest, knows how to solve problems on a city, county, state or national level, etc. In other words, they can sell him to their friends and ask for a contribution to the campaign. The members of the finance committee can direct the letter to members of their own profession and can state reasons why this candidate can do more for them if he gets elected. If done correctly, this type of letter can carry a lot of weight and get a sizeable return in contributions. Mass mailing are sent to everyone on selected lists and cannot be as specific as a personal letter; however, they can be just as effective. Lists can be obtained from local chambers of commerce, fraternal and service organization rosters, professional and trade associations, previous fundraising campaigns, church membership rosters, and lists of those registered in his own political party.

The letter can be tailored to fit the type of person included in the list showing them, for example, why the candidate should be supported by the Homeowner's Association or the Small Business Association because of his stands on previous legislation affecting them. It is a good idea to use a professional who knows how to write a letter with enough data and emotional appeal to cause the person to send a check by return mail.

Included in each mailing, whether it is a personal or mass mailing, should be a pledge card. To get the most mileage from such a card it is wise to solicit both funds and volunteers on one card. In many instances, a person will send a check and also volunteer to work at headquarters, do telephoning, etc. You can include an addressed envelope with or without a stamp. Stamps are expensive and most people will understand that they are helping to save the campaign several hundred of dollars in postage.

This can also be handled in email and donations can be handled by PayPal or credit card. SquareUp.com offers fundraising solutions that include compliant reporting functionality that is built in to their service.

Political Action Committees

A Political Action Committee (PAC) is an organization that is required to file Federal and/or State funding requirements once it has spent $1,000 or more (usually) in the pursuit of advancing an agenda or candidate(s). They are the "special interest groups" you've heard so much about, and a good source of funding if you can get it. Try www.*opensecrets.org* and search for your issue or State to find some. For State and Local races *www.followthemoney.org* provides information about donors to individual legislative and other state and local candidates and is a good source of research when building your donor target list.

Remember, just because they are reporting it, doesn't mean that you don't have to as well!

JOE GREEN FOR MAYOR COMMITTEE
P.O. BOX 1234
OURTOWN, U.S.A.

YES! I want to help elect Joe Green as Mayor of Ourtown!

Enclosed is my check for $ _____

I will pledge $ _____ to be payable on or before
_____.

I would also like to volunteer to help in the campaign. I would like to:

☐ Work in the campaign headquarters

☐ Do telephoning from my home

☐ Help canvass my neighborhood

☐ Hold a coffee or dessert

☐ Help wherever I am needed

Name (please print)

_____

Address:

_____

_____

Phone _____

Cell/Mobile _____

Email Address_____

Signature

_____

Newspaper, Radio and Television

Anytime you run a newspaper ad (up until the last week of the campaign) include a coupon, or QR Code for mobile donations that can be clipped and returned with a contribution and/or a pledge to volunteer. Many people would like to help but do not know where to call, where to send a contribution, or even how to find your office or the candidate. Letting them know that they are welcome to be a part of the campaign through contributions of time and effort may be just what they need to get involved. In these days many good people who have never been politically involved now want to become a part of getting good men and women elected to public office, but they do not know how or where to begin. Your "ad" can direct them to your candidate.

You can get the same mileage out of a radio or television spot. At the end of the "spot" when it is time for the credits, simply have the announcer say, "If you would like to send a contribution or help in any way please call 123-456-7890 (the campaign headquarters). Have the number flashed on the screen. Be sure you have someone there to answer the phone who can speak to them knowledgeably and enthusiastically. Or, if it after hours have it redirected to a mobile phone OR get a Google "voice" number than can be answered at a number of locations. You want them to immediately get their contribution in the mail or recruit them for the campaign before their excitement wears off.

The final word about fund-raising is this: Don't be afraid to ask. You may safely assume that because you are so excited about getting your candidate elected that others, if they knew him and knew what he could do, would be just as excited and generous. Give them a chance to be a part of a winning team!

11 WHY A POLITICAL TECHNO STRATEGY?

Political Techno Strategies are truly the great equalizer in American politics.

Whether you are a prospective candidate, already elected, a social activist, a volunteer, a 99% Occupy Guy or a Tea Partying Instigator—having a solid grasp of, and being ever informed of, best practices when it comes to "Electronic Campaigning" is crucial.

We have at our fingertips, Websites, Social Media, Group Thinking and Online Collaboration via email, or web conferencing, Mobile Marketing and Alerts, infographics, YouTube and geographic and demographically database identified voter targets. It seems everyday brings a technological advancement in communication that can benefit a political strategy.

Force Multiplication with the stroke of a key.

With a basic knowledge, and some inside tips, you can be successful whether you have millions of 527 dollars to spend, or are collecting donations at $5 a pop via mobile donations!

For the most part the tools are available and easy to use. They are tools which enable you to ENGAGE and ACTIVATE.

It is important that you treat your online/digital campaign as an extension of yourself. It is not simply an electronic brochure or leaflet. It is an opportunity for your campaign to be out front 24/7.

It doesn't take a genius to read the numbers. More and more we are tethered to our computers and mobile devices as our days seem to get shorter and shorter and our responses faster and faster. If you aren't engaging the voter or supporter "WHERE THEY LIVE"—you're missing the boat.

The web, mobile and social media afford you the opportunity to engage the disengaged populace.

This isn't a joke, but when in doubt, ask a 15 year old to help you define your strategy!

If the mantra of Real Estate is "location, location, location", then the mantra of online campaigning and politics in general is "Engage, Engage, Engage."

The following chapters outline some of the basic strategies you might deploy in developing your successful Political Techno Strategy. Things change quickly in terms of sites, trends and tactics. Staying on top of them can get you distracted from your goal.

If you simply keep in mind that you are using the technology to your advantage by ENGAGING your constituents, technology will serve you, versus you serving technology.

Still water gathers moss, rolling stones turn into snowballs—and sometimes an avalanche. (Or is that still water runs deep; rolling stones gather no moss and politics makes strange bedfellows? Yikes!) Pick your own cliché and run with it.

Always remember—no matter what marketing strategy you deploy, even saying "hi" to someone in the grocery store line WILL be Googled (searched).

It is of the utmost importance that you (a) participate and therefore (b) do your best to control your message, image and hopefully growing importance and supporter base.

12 WEBSITE AND SEARCH ENGINE OPTIMIZATION

Less than 10 years ago very few political campaigns and issue based organizations even had a website. These days your website is mission critical to your success. In fact, your website can *solve* a lot of the communication, data collection, fundraising, management of volunteers and Get Out the Vote deployment challenges. There are a variety of cost and functionality options that you may consider. As with just about everything covered in this book, visit *www.guidetowinningelections.com* for more information about all of these topics, especially technology and voter strategies which seem to change and become more efficient almost daily!

TYPES OF WEBSITE

A Hosted Solution such as NationBuilder (see the chapter on "Campaign Management Software" for more information). These solutions are highly functional and cost effective in terms of their out of the box services such as fund raising tools like moneybombs and crowdfunding to social network integration and text message marketing.

A Self Hosted solution such as WordPress. WordPress is an open source Content Management System that is highly extensible and with a very large and active support and add-on development community. There is a large selection of cost effective and free themes available and design work can be quite affordable. Consider integrating voter management software like Trail Blazer with your WordPress, Joomla or HTML site to leverage converting those browsers into contributors, voters and supporters.

Every political website should have at least the following:

DESIGN TIPS

In the United States, almost every political candidate website seems to revolve around the colors red, white and blue which makes sense. But those aren't the only colors that can help with your audience—example: if you are targeting women voters, consider pinks and pastels as highlight colors, or issue specific highlights. Use lots of images, and video if you have it, and if you have *action oriented* options such as donations, register, signup with Facebook/Google+, volunteer, etc. place them "above the fold" (so viewers can see them without scrolling down). Make sure your site is easy to navigate (get around) and that you don't completely overwhelm the visitor with clutter.

ABOUT/BIO/PLATFORM

Clearly state your purpose, your positions and policies, your history and your goals. You don't have to overdo it. Use your platform to ENGAGE potential supporters, contributors, and voters. Break out your Platform in your navigation so that your TOP issues each have their own "page" and corresponding link either in the form of drop down menus, sidebars or in a top level page entitled "Issues" or "Platform" whereby visitors can see your overall truncated positions, but with the ability to click for the expanded explanation. Example:

> ***Gun Control:*** *Candidate X supports the 2nd Amendment to the Constitution and an individual's right to bear arms, but is also concerned about safety in our schools and communities. READ MORE about Candidate X's position on Gun Control.* The READ MORE is an **active link** to the full, expanded explanation of the candidate's position.

LOGIN/REGISTER

In many cases, especially if you are planning a data-driven campaign, it is smart to enable your website with login/registration functionality. This can range from asking them to register with their email address, or in many cases and better yet, with their Facebook, Google+ or Twitter account. Encouraging your visitors and supporters to "register" in any and all formats will help you better communicate with them, raise more money and spread the word across social networks to the friends and families of your supporters more rapidly and effectively.

VOLUNTEER/DONATE

Raising money online and capturing as much data as possible is an essential component of a successful campaign. You should incorporate donation and volunteering options/solutions on your website (and for mobile/tablet devices). See the "Online Fundraising" chapter for more information.

EVENT SCHEDULE

Your site should have an updatable campaign schedule which highlights all of your events, and if possible, be interactive to accept reservations and contributions in the case of fundraising breakfasts or dinners. If possible your schedule should also be *integratable* with your social media and other digital media tools.

CONTACT INFORMATION

Make it easy for people to contact your campaign via every possible mechanism—phone, mail, email, contact form, social media, mobile and any other possible way you can think of utilizing! Make sure you capture every piece of data possible so that you can analyze, manipulate and deploy the most effective communication and fundraising tactics. This is especially true with web based contact forms, always double check that, however you set up your forms, you have access to the data in a usable format.

RESPONSIVE DESIGN

What this means is simply that your website is viewable/actionable across a variety of platforms and devices—computer, pad/tablet, mobile device, etc. There are differing levels of "responsiveness" with the best being a fully self-standing mobile designed template/theme to simply using a "responsive" WordPress theme as the back-end content management system of your site. StudioPress has a variety of cost effective and reasonably responsive WordPress themes if you are on a budget.

LEGAL COMPLIANCE

Don't forget to comply with local and State election laws regarding campaigning, such as when you are legally allowed to begin campaigning, can you use the word "elect" or not, adherence to campaign fundraising laws, disclosure and reporting requirements, whether or not your State/Locality considers certain web based activities to be "in kind contributions" or not, etc. Most States and the FEC will provide this information online and up to date.

13 ONLINE ADVERTISING

Online advertising can get pretty complicated on the paid side. It's good to have someone on your team that understands how to spend your budget correctly. And there *is* a correct way to spend it! Blindly spending $10,000 on paid advertising probably won't get the job done. Paying a specialist, or a member of your team $1,000 will probably save you $5,000 on every $10,000.

One thing to always consider is "In Kind" advertising. Always check with your Federal, State and Local registrars and election bodies about creative marketing and the financing laws which might apply to website owners offering to provide your campaign with "free" advertising. It's sort of a grey area, but not one you want to be the first to get busted for leveraging!

Here's an overview and some common sense strategies.

AdWords, Bing and other Traditional Online Advertising

Google AdWords is arguably the most popular and widespread form of online advertising available to political candidates. For those that don't know, Google AdWords are the ads that show up on the "results page" of a Google Search. They also show up on millions of websites across the Internet that serve up advertisements via the Google AdSense program.

The AdWords program is essentially an "auction" site of available space on Google and the websites of its "partners." This advertising could be anything from an individual blog to a major news destination. You select the search keywords for which you would like your ad to appear, create an "approved" ad, and then bid for position on the search results page against the "competition."

See http://www.google.com/ads/elections/

In 2008 *Obama for America* spent close to $20 million in online advertising, while McCain spent approximately $4 million.

Retargeting/Remarketing

The simplest definition of "Retargeting" or "Behavioral Retargeting" is that your ad gets shown over a variety of subscriber networks more often to visitors who have previously visited your website. This is accomplished by installing a "code snippet" usually in the form of a "pixel" (a very small piece of code that doesn't interfere with your website) across your website, or on specific pages. As the "previous visitor" continues to navigate the Internet, your ad appears on various and sundry sites which are part of the network.

Retargeting can be a useful and cost effective way to continuously engage your potential supporters. Beware though, at some point, you might drive them away. This is not to say that you shouldn't use retargeting throughout the length of your campaign.

If you have a limited budget, or just feel like implementing your own strategy, there are several vendors that can help out with that and their "support" teams are experienced and helpful when getting you set up.

If you are planning a significant online strategy of any sort, and even more important direct mail, TV, Radio, etc. retargeting/remarketing should be a significant portion of your overall spend. Remember, almost EVERYTHING you do in your campaign will result in a direct website visit, or a Google or Bing search. *Retargeting maximizes your original spend, with minimal additional cost.*

If you have a larger budget, and need a more targeted, precise solution, there are highly qualified and effective consulting firms such as Campaign Grid (http://www.campaigngrid.com) that provide truly cutting edge solutions that incorporate highly targeted advertising to online, mobile and video audiences. You can probably do this on your own, but these guys have it nailed.

CampaignGrid's platform enables you to target only registered voters with over 100 different data segments across 90% of all websites. These types of solutions are potential game changers in terms of cost-effectiveness and success rates. For example: you could segment registered Republicans that voted in the last election, who donated money in a specific State House District and serve up to them your "Fundraising Message."

Here are some of the potential ways retargeting can enhance your campaign results:

Raising Money—find new donors, thank online donors, promote a money bomb or fundraising event

- Get Out The Vote—remind them to exercise their purchase, especially significant for off-year elections, issue advocacy/lobbying and local elections such as bond issues, or school districts.

- Name ID/Campaign Recognition—get them to know your name.

- Grassroots/Volunteer Organization—develop your supporter lists, recruit volunteers, promote events.

- Voter Education/Issue Advocacy—keep your supporters engaged, attract new supporters for specific initiatives, generate calls to action

There are essentially 7 types of Retargeting that are useful for political and advocacy campaigns.

1. Site Retargeting

The concept of Site Retargeting is simple. A visitor to your site sees YOUR AD across various networks (millions of sites) when they visit those sites in the future, for a specific period of time. For example: I visit Joe Citizen for Mayor's website. I then venture on to my local TV or newspaper website, or to almost any major web destination that displays advertising, and BOOM there is Joe Citizen for Mayor's ad reminding to me vote on Tuesday. This is repeated over and over again across millions of websites only showing up when I get there, and only "paid for" when a previous visitor views the ad.

Your retargeting campaign can also be segmented based upon which pages of your site the visitor viewed. For example: If the visitor went to your Donate page, but didn't make a donation, that visitor might get a "Support Joe Citizen, Donate Now"—or "Come to Our BBQ Fundraiser" advertisement versus an issue based ad like "Support Our Police—Vote Joe".

Site retargeting has recently been introduced via Facebook Exchange enabling your advertisements to appear across the popular social network to their members who have previously visited your site.

2. Search Retargeting

The principle here is essentially the same, except that your ads are "retargeted" to individuals who have searched for a specific keyword or for phrases that pertain to your campaign or issue. Search retargeting is less precise than site, email, CRM or other forms of retargeting as you are not able to determine the level of interest or the intent of the searcher. "5th Congressional District California" doesn't necessarily mean the searcher is interested in donating to your campaign, or learning about your position on the Department of Education.

Consider that the searcher probably doesn't want to see a ton of ads for "Donate Now" if they were really just trying to find the Congressional Staffer who can help them with their visit to Washington, or to buy a flag that flew over the Capitol. Be strategic when crafting your search retargeting message.

If you are willing to do the work, or your contracted firm has the capability, you can fine tune your search remarketing by combining the search term used to land on your site with what they do once they get there, and craft your message accordingly. CampaignGrid, Retargeter and AdRoll are suggested firms. Google is trying to get their own thing going.

3. Relationship Retargeting

This one takes a little more work, but can be highly successful if properly deployed. This actually seems one of the most logical ways to use online advertising, yet isn't often deployed as it is "outside of the box" of most platform developers and their Cost Per Thousand revenue models.

Relationship Retargeting can be closely compared to having a relative, friendly or supportive website owner place your retargeting pixel on their site in order to "retarget" your advertisements to their website visitors. Here are two examples.

Example 1: Political Candidate

You've won the primary so it is time to place your pixel on all of the Party Related sites in your District/State. You could take it a step further and engage your supporters to place your pixel as well. Keep in mind that you will want to keep up to date with Federal Election Commission regulations on Coordinated Communications and applying appropriate donor/in-kind information and limits as well to all Federal Elections. Individual states may also have limits and restrictions so check our website for more information: http://guidetowinningelections.com/

The future of campaign communications, especially electronically, is developing rapidly, and many tactics haven't been reviewed or even brought up with regard to regulation, and most will probably be challenged in the Courts.

It's best to err on the side of caution and keep good records. Most Retargeting service providers deliver highly detailed information about your campaigns which can assist if you need to produce records.

Here's a link to the FEC's brochure regarding Coordinate Communications:

http://www.fec.gov/pages/brochures/indexp.shtml

Example 2: Issue Oriented

A referendum is on the county ballot to add a new, higher tax category specifically for real estate investors, i.e. all non-owner occupied residential real estate. This means that a higher property tax will be required on the cabin you have in the woods, or those two townhouses you rent out, or that real estate prices might diminish as investors decide to take their money elsewhere in order to avoid the additional expense.

Your organization is against the referendum. In order to effectuate your campaign you place your pixel on the websites of every real estate agent in your County, every hardware store, every title and mortgage company and on the sites of friendly local business organizations such as the Chamber of Commerce or the State and Local Real Estate Associations.

The visitors to those sites will then see, and hopefully act, upon your ads which are then shown on approximately 90% of the websites that accept advertising.

4. *CRM* (Customer Relationship Management) Retargeting

CRM Retargeting applies the same retargeting principles, but is based upon your existing database of supporters, donors, voters, etc. and can be similarly deployed with differing messages and calls to action throughout your campaign.

5. Email Retargeting

Email Retargeting affords you the ability to retarget individuals who have had some sort of action/engagement with your campaign via email. You can retarget them based upon which link they might have clicked, whether they opened the email, etc. Email retargeting is effective when combined with coordinated display advertising.

14 DATABASE ACQUISITION AND MANAGEMENT

The most valuable commodity I know of is information.
- Gordon Gekko, Wall Street (1987)

Whether or not you think Oliver Stone's Gordon Gekko was a genius or a well of creepiness, his comment is correct, especially when it comes to leveraging voter, volunteer and donor data.

Most states/counties will, usually for a fee, provide you with a list that has at least this basic data set: voter name, residence address, mailing address if different, party registration, race, gender, registration date and last voting date. This is usually your starting point, but certainly not where you want to end up!

A winning campaign is based upon the "value" and "use" of its data. There are 3 C's to campaign data:

CORRECTNESS

People move, change parties, drop dead, have a criminal conviction, are declared mentally incompetent, change their name because of divorce or marriage, turn 18 or register for the first time. Getting the correct data from the start is the crucial launch point for your voter, volunteer, supporter and donor campaigns. There are a variety of means to acquire these lists, which we will discuss below.

COST

Depending upon your budget, your "marketing" strategy, the geographic scope of the office you are seeking and how you intend to deploy the data in the hands of your volunteers, your cost can vary from ZERO to tens of thousands of dollars.

CURRENT

Let's assume that you started with an up-to-date list. A lot of things happen between the start of your campaign, and 18 months later when the election actually happens. Other than the obvious address changes, new voters, etc. you will have, and had better take, the opportunity to update and enhance your database at every contact with a voter, volunteer, supporter or contributor. Take advantage of these contacts by appending your database with additional "data fields" and get creative. In your Campaign Management Software, or Contact Management Software add fields such as:

- *Issue Interests*—create dropdowns, or checkboxes to identify the issue interests of individual voters. This will allow you to target specific voters with the appropriate message that interests them.

- *Profession*—a small business owner likely has different interests and hot buttons than college student and a corporate manager will have different concerns than a truck driver.

- *Children/Marital Status:* Often overlooked is collecting usable data regarding a voters family—usually their number one issue, or at least the "Rome" to which all roads lead. Drill this down as far as possible. Example: You've collected the information that Joe Voter is a single father of three, divorced. You probably don't want to send Joe an email outlining your position that you support revoking his driver's license if he misses or is short on one child support payment, **or** Joe Voter is married with three kids, named Joe, Jr., Susie, and Bobbie. You do want to send Joe that mailer reminding him of your position on School Vouchers and "merge" in "to help Joe, Jr., Susie and Bobbie best prepare for their future."

The key to maximizing the effectiveness of your database is DISCIPLINE. Make sure you are doing it yourself, and train your workers to do the same.

Utilize technology as best you can, and can afford, to make it as easy as possible to collect and add new data. This can range from simply having a data entry volunteer punch it all in, to providing your precinct workers Tablet Computers to update on the fly as they go door to door, stand

117

outside the Library or work an event.

Consider your database a living animal that needs to be fed constantly and fed well.

Track and Log All of Your Contacts—depending upon the Campaign Management Software, or system, you are deploying you will want to create some way of tracking and logging all of your contacts with voters, supporters, volunteers and contributors. You don't want to bombard contributors with Donation Requests if they just gave yesterday, and you want to manipulate, control and diversify your issue messages to potential voters, contributors and supporters.

COMPLETNESS

If you're properly tracking and logging all your contacts, your database will grow in completeness and effectiveness. If you have the money, you can dramatically advance the timeline by "appending" additional data fields to your database. There are many firms out there that can provide this information and append it to your database—then add the new data to match up with the old data.

Many data fields can be appended these days ranging from Linkedin profiles, Facebook or Twitter, to even targeting the mobile network. Companies such as CampaignGrid (www.campaigngrid.com) have over 100 different data fields that can supplement and enhance your database, marketing, GOTV (get out the vote)and fundraising efforts.

Finding the Right Voter Lists

From the Government: As a candidate, or valid political organization, you should be able to acquire basic voter lists from your State's Secretary of State's office or from your local elections board or bureau (usually the County). All States/Counties will provide the list to political candidates, and some States have unrestricted voter lists available for any organization. Costs will vary by State or locality—example: Washington State will provide you with a monthly updated CD-ROM for $7 a month versus Maryland which offers the whole State for $125 plus some handling charges, but gives you the option to contact your local election bureau to obtain smaller and less expensive lists.

From the Party: If you're running as a major party candidate the party has a good list, usually with a lot more information that what is included on the government lists. It's a good idea to check with them as well. If you're running in a contested primary the party may or may not share their in-house lists with any candidate (except the incumbent probably already has the same, or better data). Once you win the primary and become the "official" candidate in the general election, the party shouldn't have a problem sharing their data with you. Remember that the Party is a private organization and doesn't have to share with you if they don't want to do so.

Always keep in mind, especially if you're new on the scene, that this is POLITICS and everybody has a favorite and an opinion. YOUR list, if built and maintained properly, should always be the best.

List Brokers: If you have the money, you might decide to go with a political list broker to outright buy a complete list to start with, or to add new data by appending it to your existing list. Costs vary based upon the quality of the list. Always make sure that whatever you're buying is updated against the National Change of Address database, and preferably against the most recent State/Locality voter registration database before you append anything and end up with a slew of duplicates that you'll then have to parse out.

Always get the list in a digital format, usually a .csv, .txt or Excel file.

Using the List

Other than the obvious—mail and phone—you might want to segment your list out for different uses depending upon your data. Email and mobile are separately addressed later in this book. Following is one that's incredibly important!

Street Lists and How to Use Them

Simply put, Street Lists are broken down and organized versions of your voter list segmented for door-to-door campaigning either by yourself or volunteers. Here are some street list ideas to make life easier on you and your volunteers.

Break down the list by each side of the street separately, and block by block if possible to make a "walking list" for those going door-to-door. This makes it easier for them to maximize their time and accurately record information as they walk along. If you're using a political list broker, they'll break it down for you in regular and "walk" formats if you ask.

There are a variety of enhanced technologies you can deploy here ranging from 4G tablet solutions to simply getting large precinct maps and lists from the Country Registrar or Election Bureau. These solutions change fast and new solutions are appearing constantly, keep up with them on www.guidetowinningelections.com.

What to do with my list if I lose? We all hope to win our election and prevail in our advocacy pursuits, but not everyone can win. Here are some things to consider if you find yourself "out of the race."

Your list has value and you paid for it in blood, sweat, tears and hard earned dollars.

You are still a player, especially if you lost in the primary. Don't give your list away without some sort of "compensation"—just like you wouldn't give away your prime sign locations or sign posts. If you've lost the primary and you're still friendly with your opponent, support him/her in the General Election with some list sharing. You'll make new friends for your next election campaign.

Immediately change all of the accessible passwords to your database and do a full backup onto a DVD(s) or up to the Cloud or a Server that you control —you should have been doing backups and storing in a safe place or third party system along the way anyhow.

You might decide to run again, or have an issue that's important to you and your supporters. It's not a bad idea to keep in touch with your base, even if you have no intention of running for office in the future.

ALWAYS send a thank you after the campaign, **especially if you lost**. You might also need the list to help settle some campaign debts, either through raising funds after the election, or possibly by "selling/renting" the list to another campaign. **CAVEAT:** Here's where the question of your "Privacy Policy" comes into play. If you told everyone that you "won't sell or rent their information to anyone," don't. It's your privacy policy, create one from the beginning that suits your needs, and run it by an attorney, then follow it.

Remember that you might be able to parlay the value of your database to help out key workers that might need to transition to another campaign. They won't forget that one!

15 SOCIAL MEDIA

Social Media has become the latest, highly effective tool for campaign, candidate and issue advocacy, and for some good reasons.

- It's cost effective.
- Like minded individuals can easily join up and participate.
- It's viral. Years ago there was a shampoo commercial that deployed the tagline "And they told 2 friends, and they told 2 friends and so on, and so on, and so on." We used to call it "Word of Mouth"—now we call it social networking and it pervades all forms of communication.

Here are some numbers from a 2012 Pew Research Center study:

69% of American Adults use social networks
66% use Facebook
16% use Twitter
22% of Registered Voters shared their Presidential votes on social media
38% say they "like" or promote materials about political or social issues posted by other people
35% have used social networks to encourage other people to vote
34% have posted their own thoughts on political or social issues
28% have used social networks to post links to articles or news about political issues or candidates
20% have used social networks to follow candidates or elected officials
12% have used Facebook to get their political news (this number **doubled** during the 2012 campaign).

Source: Pew Research Center, November 29, 2012

(http://pewInternet.org/Infographics/2012/Digital-Politics.aspx)

Here's a great example that happened to me by accident and is perfect example of how things go viral.

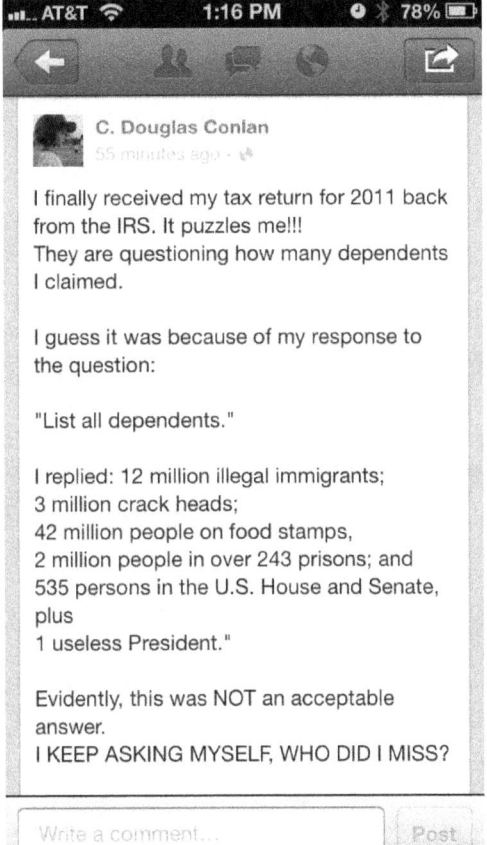

As I was writing this chapter this happened. A colleague of mine sent me an email that I thought was funny

I copied the email and posted it to my personal Facebook Page.

20 minutes later an acquaintance of mine from high school 20 years ago received it on his mobile phone, took a screen shot of his phone and re-posted it to his Facebook Page and sent it as a graphic to his phone list.

It went from email to Facebook to Mobile back to Facebook in 20 minutes.

Not only did the email then go out to my 300 Facebook friends, but also to my high school acquaintance's 892 friends!

And it went further with likes and comments and copies and shares, reaching well over 3,000 individuals in less than 12 hours.

Facebook

In case you didn't know, Facebook is the world's largest social networking site (and probably the 3rd largest Country in the world) with over 1 Billion users worldwide. Approximately half of Facebook's users utilize a mobile device to access the site and communicate with friends, associates and organizations.

Having a Facebook presence is obligatory for any political campaign or issue oriented movement. Since Facebook is an advertising supported company you don't really need to spend a lot of money on your Facebook campaign.

There are however, "Apps" which you might look at adding to extend the functionality of your site. An App is essentially anything you want to "happen" on your Facebook page—donations, volunteer signups, extensible calendars, and polling. There are a slew of free Facebook applications that are easy to configure and install, as well as cost effective out-of-the-box solutions and, of course, you can always pay someone to write you something completely unique.

For the benefit of your campaign, Facebook has a Politics & Government Team at https://www.facebook.com/uspolitics. Click on "Contact Us" and the team will get in touch. They also have a downloadable handbook on Best Practices.

To follow are some things that you want to keep in mind to achieve the best results on Facebook.

GETTING STARTED

There are some basics you need to know to get started.

1. *Personal Profile versus Page.* In order to use Facebook, you first have to sign up as an individual. Once that is accomplished you will want to setup a "Page" specifically for your campaign. It might be a good idea, especially if the candidate has already established a Faceook presence, to "hide" the Personal Profile during the campaign so that you don't confuse voters.

2. *Vanity URL*—you will want to set up your "vanity URL" as quickly as possible (you need 25 "likes" to secure your vanity URL). Example: http://facebook.com/yourname. It's probably a better idea to simply use your name versus your name and office because in the future you might be running for another office which would essentially make your old vanity URL look rather silly and you can't just pick up and move.

3. *Use the Timeline* to tell your story. Facebook allows you to add information, pictures, and video to your timeline going all the way back to 1800. Use this space to tell your WHOLE story.

4. *Add some apps.* You can essentially have three. Standard practice is to include Like Us, Donate and Volunteer, but there is room to get creative.

5. *Customize your cover photo* to 850 pixels by 315 pixels. Ideally this should match the look and feel of your campaign, and website. A good place to go for help on this one, and other little things is www.fiverr.com where you can get a custom Facebook cover photo done for $5. There are a lot of good deals on Fivrr if you're working with a limited budget.

RUNNING YOUR FACEBOOK CAMPAIGN

1. Try to post at least once every day. There is a feature that allows you to schedule your posts ahead of time, which also allows you to target the peak times you want your message delivered/posted. According to some studies, the best time to reach your audience appears to be between 9 and 10 PM, presumably after the dishes are done and the kids are in bed.

2. Post in your own conversational voice and try to include a picture with each of your posts. Posts with pictures receive twice the engagement that text-only posts receive.

3. If you have the budget, consider using Facebook Advertising to promote your campaign. These are cost effective and highly targetable.

4. Engage your audience with something to do, or at least get them involved in the conversation. Here's a good place to do a poll application or use Facebook Questions to start a dialogue.

5. Use video, either pre-recorded, or using Facebook's new live video functionality.

6. Use Facebook Insights to help you understand your audience for better engagement.

7. When you are promoting your Facebook page it's better to use the www.facebook.com/yourname versus simply a "Like us on Facebook" icon in your print, television and other advertising.

8. Make it easy for supporters to share your information, encourage their friends and family to engage your campaign and of course encourage them to "like" and "comment" on your posts.

9. "Pin" important information at the top of your timeline. Facebook allows you to "pin," or keep at the top, posts/images/videos versus getting pushed down the page with each new post. You can "pin" something for 7 days, or until you "pin" the next item.

10. DON'T cross post your Tweets to Facebook and vice versa. They operate in a different way, and you'll end up hitting your people with the same message in many cases with duplicates. If you want to simplify the whole process try HootSuite or Sprout Social to manage your multiple social networks, schedule posts and more.

Linkedin

Linkedin is a social networking site with over 200 million members worldwide specifically designed around the needs of professionals. Although it is a social network, Linkedin works a little bit differently than Facebook or Twitter. Linkedin has the potential for several political campaign uses.

1. *Fundraising.* The demographics of the average Linkedin user is most likely among the top in terms of household income and education.

2. *Groups.* Join groups that are related to your campaign. Business verticals which are likely inclined to your point of view, religious or political groups, and of course, anything local to your district.

3. *Endorsements.* Use Linkedin to get endorsements for your candidate or campaign.

4. *Recruit:* Use Linkedin to find staffers or interns and volunteers.

TWITTER

Twitter is most definitely the world's most popular "alert system"—although it has become a bit more of a phenomenon that just 160 characters of "Just stopping by the store, don't call me right now!"

The value of Twitter in actually winning elections is probably too early to call. What we do know is that the Obama campaign out-tweeted Romney by an 8-1 ratio. We do know that Twitter cannot be ignored.

So what are your options for leveraging Twitter to your advantage?

How it Works (According to Twitter—pretty much verbatim)
What are Political Ads?

Political Ads are advertising campaigns purchased by political advertisers in order to reach a wider audience or engage current followers on Twitter. These ads may include Promoted Tweets, Promoted Accounts, or Promoted Trends.

Political Ads function in the exact same way as campaigns run by other advertisers on Twitter.

How can I tell if I'm seeing a Political Ad?

Like other ads on Twitter, Political Ads are clearly labeled as Promoted with a Promoted icon and information about who has purchased the Ad.

You can tell if a Promoted Tweet, Account, or Trend on Twitter is a Political Ad by the purple Promoted icon that appears below or next to the advertisement.

Hovering or mousing over the "Promoted by" text to the right of the Promoted icon will display a bubble showing what organization paid for the advertising campaign. Users accessing Twitter from a mobile device or official Twitter app will not be able to hover over Political Ads. However, the advertising account's Twitter profile will include a link to a website with more information about the organization.

See the ad below:

Who can run Political Ad campaigns?

Political Ads are run by candidates and their political committees who are advocating for the election or defeat of a candidate for public office.

Twitter currently only offers Political Ads to political advertisers within the United States.

What are the policies for political ads?

As with all advertisers, political campaigns are responsible for all their promoted content, which includes complying with applicable laws and regulations regarding online advertisements. Political ads must also comply with all Promoted Products policies, and Twitter is responsive to complaints about violations of policy. In particular, political ads may not promote hate or "anti" concepts or speech, or advocate against an individual or protected group. Please note that standard political discourse, such as promoting an issue, advocating against a candidate's stance, or general advocacy against a candidate's election, may be acceptable and is generally not considered hate speech.

Infographics

Infographics are the combination of pictures, text and hopefully verified data that portend to induce the recipient to take action, change their mind or at least think about a partisan issue.

There are essentially 3 types of Infographics that can be effectively used by campaigns, activists and issue oriented advocacy groups and ballot referendums.

The Candidate Infographic:

The Talking Point Infographic:

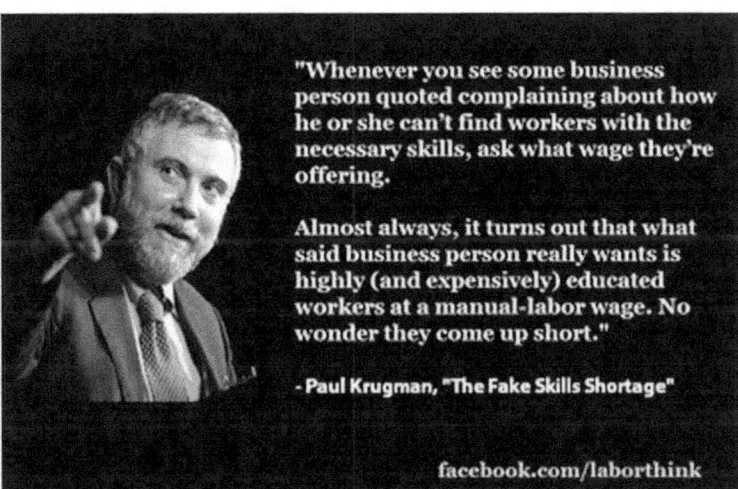

The Numbers and Sense Infographic

Combining the visual with fact based numbers gives online, and, potentially, mobile users a quick overview and call to action on a specific issue, referendum or candidate's position.

Here are some important things to consider:

1. Make sure your facts are correct. Remember, this is going to go viral so verify, verify, verify and cite your sources. You don't want to get caught with fudged numbers which might damage your credibility, or distract from your message.

2. **ALWAYS** include online, and offline if applicable, ways for the "viewer" to contact you.

3. Use specific calls to action to mobilize your supporters, increase donations or volunteers or direct viewers to "learn more" or "watch the video".

5. Distribution: simply sticking the infographic on Pinterest or WeHeartIt isn't going to produce the desired results. Utilize your social networks, email and supporter lists to go "viral" with your message. Educate and Encourage your supporters to spread the word.

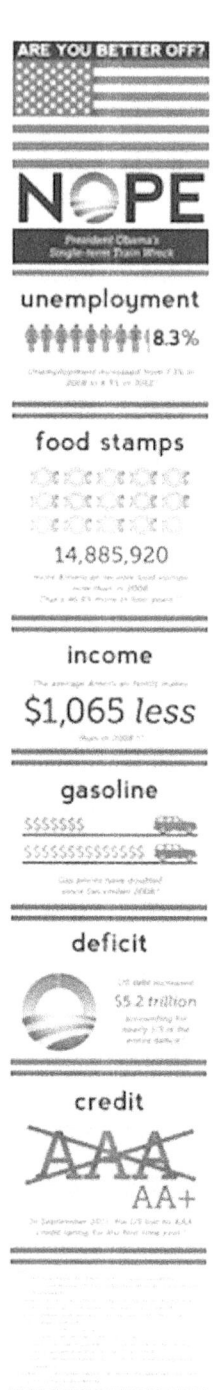

The "Numbers & Sense" Infographic can be successfully deployed by candidates, advocacy and issue groups and in support of specific calls to action such as "Email Your Congressman" or "Donate/Join Now."

We've compiled and continuously add new and innovative infographics to our database for your review.

http://guidetowinningelections.com/ political-advertising/political-infographics/

YOUTUBE AND ON LINE VIDEO

If a picture is worth a thousand words, then video is worth a million, and viral video in the social space, worth even more.

An October 2012 Pew Research study related to the 2012 election campaign found that among registered voters who go online:

- 48% watch video news reports about the election or politics.

- 40% watch previously recorded videos of candidate speeches, press conferences, or debates.

- 39% watch informational videos online that explain a political issue.

- 37% watch humorous or parody videos dealing with political issues.

- 36% watch political advertisements online.

- 28% watch live videos of candidate speeches, press conferences, or debates.

All told, two thirds (66%) of Internet-using registered voters watched one or more of the above political videos online during the 2012 campaign. Voters who have given "quite a lot" of thought to the election are especially likely to watch political videos online. Some 73% of these individuals have watched online political videos this election season, compared with 45% of those who say that they have been following the campaign less closely.

What types of political videos are voters watching?

All percentages based on registered voters who use the internet within each group

	All RV's who go online (n=721)	Republican (n=203)	Democrat (n=224)	Independent (n=261)
Video news reports about the election or politics	48%	44%	52%	47%
Previously recorded video of a candidate speech, press conference or debate	40	37	43	40
Informational videos that explain a political issue	39	38	38	41
Humorous or parody videos dealing with political issues	37	33	40	39
Political advertisements	36	38	37	34
Live video of a candidate speech, press conference or debate	28	24	30	27
Total ("yes" to any of the above activities)	66	64	69	65

Source: Pew Research Center's Internet & American Life Project, Omnibus Survey, October 12-14, 2012. N=1,006 adults ages 18 and older, including 400 interviews conducted on respondent's cell phone. The survey was conducted in English. Margin of error is +/-4.4 percentage points for internet users who are registered voters (n=721).

http://www.pewInternet.org/Reports/2012/Election-2012-Video/Main-Report/Online-Videos-and-Campaign-2012.aspx

Some 62% of Internet-using registered voters have had other people recommend online videos for them to watch related to the election or politics this campaign season. Specifically:

40% have had other people recommend election or politics-related online videos for them to watch by posting them on a social networking site.

36% have had other people recommend election or politics-related online videos by telling them about them in person.

32% have had other people recommend election or politics-related online videos by sending an email or text message.

Online video recommendations from others

% of registered voters who use the internet who have had other people recommend online videos related to politics or the election for them to watch by...

	Posting them on a social networking site	Telling you about them in person	Sending you an email or text message
Total for RV's who use the internet (n=721)	40%	36%	32%
Party ID			
Republicans (n=203)	39	36	34
Democrats (n=224)	47	41	31
Independents (n=261)	33	32	32
Party ID (w/ leaners)			
Republicans + Rep-leaning Independents (n=334)	37	35	35
Democrats + Dem-leaning Independents (n=320)	45	39	32
Ideology			
Liberal (n=137)	53**	38	33
Moderate (n=278)	38	36	32
Conservative (n=283)	35	36	33

Source: Pew Research Center's Internet & American Life Project, Omnibus Survey, October 12-14, 2012. N=1,006 adults ages 18 and older, including 400 interviews conducted on respondent's cell phone. The survey was conducted in English. Margin of error is +/-4.4 percentage points for internet users who are registered voters (n=721). **Indicates that figure is significantly larger than all other rows in group.

In this day and age there is going to be video—either productions of your own, productions by others, and most likely video created by people in the "audience." You can control your own productions, but you can't control what the competition might do. You might be able to control, at least mitigate what the audience might do—keeping in mind that many mobile users can record and immediately distribute over social networks, email and text anything they just recorded.

You can have a strategy that successfully addresses all three.

Creating, Scripting, Production Mechanics, Cost and Traditional Media Buying are all arts in and of themselves. Technology is rapidly affording increased capacity for campaign self-reliance, and sometimes self-destruction (there have been plenty of recent examples of "missteps" that went viral and tanked a campaign. www.guidetowinningelections.com is replete with resources for this tricky business!

Let's talk about EYEBALLS and ENGAGEMENT. If no one sees it, and it doesn't reinforce or change minds, then your Return on Investment is most likely in the red.

DISTRIBUTION

Video Viewership is ubiquitous regardless of the delivery medium—broadcast, email, video sharing sites, social networks, mobile—voters watch TV!

Video Sharing Sites—YouTube and Vimeo dominate the video space, so it is obvious that you must have a presence there. There are probably 20 or so additional video sharing sites that are worth taking the time, or spending some money through which to distribute your video. For a small investment (less that $100 a video) you can distribute across all of the networks.

Once your video is "hosted" on these networks, their users/viewers are able to share, comment, "like," embed (they put your video on their "site"—a website, their Facebook Page, etc.)

When establishing these accounts, and uploading your videos it is important to remember that each and every page, category, and individual piece of media is a stand alone "searchable" asset. Fill in all of the blanks on your profile, channels, video descriptions, social networks, etc. Be consistent with your profile descriptions, always include a link to your campaign website and use the same "profile photo" across all networks.

When uploading your videos always create topic specific Titles, Descriptions and Tags/Keywords. If you need help figuring out what are the good keywords, use Google AdWords Keyword Tool. You can get the basics for free, and much better information if you have an AdWords account.

Social Networking Sites—it should be obvious that you want to share your video on your Facebook Page, etc. That's a good starting point, and MANDATORY!.

16 ONLINE FUNDRAISING

For overview purposes, we will include mobile, tablet and social media based fundraising along with online and email in our evaluation of the marketplace.

In the 2012 President Election, Obama accomplished the following in terms of Digital Fundraising:

- $690 million out of $1 Billion raised (doesn't include Third Party Groups)

- 45 million "likes" on Facebook definitely helped their social media fundraising

- The campaign's social network for supporters "Dashboard" helped to organize and promote nearly 360,000 events with over 1.1 million RSVP's to those events

- Over 1 million people downloaded the campaign's Facebook App resulting in 600,000 supporters sharing information with an estimated 5,000,000 individual targets.

As we move toward the next election cycle, nearly every electronic device from computer to phone to ATM to your paycheck will officially become a political fundraising device (if you're a union member or supporter of an organization that takes monthly "dues" from you then you understand!).

Our "communication" obsession presents a whole new set of opportunities to raise money for political campaigns of all sorts. The $1,000 check has now become 200 $5 email or Facebook or Twitter solicitations, something over the phone, while you're speaking to them face to face or on TV, or QR Response Code donations! If you don't know what a QR code is, Google it, or get one for free at www.guidetowinningelections.com.

There are a variety of ways you actually get charged for these donations, similar to merchant fees if you were a retail store. Don't always go for the lowest percentage. You might find some value added firms that charge the same or less, but proactively work toward your success for little or no additional fees. SquareUp.com has a contribution model specifically designed for political campaigns, replete with reporting and decent rates.

You have to shake the tree to get the money. The "online/interactive" tree is growing faster than the blood of tyrants can fuel it! Thomas Jefferson would have a PayPal account and his own mobile app!

Speaking of "mobile apps"—you probably don't need one as long as your website is "responsive" and adaptable to most mobile devices. Just gear your fundraising and GOTV messages to where you want them to go!

The simplest way to start a no/low cost online fundraising campaign is to start with your friends and family, and then ask them to ask their friends, using email and mobile to direct them to your contribution page/site.

There is a great line from the genius Eric Begosian play "Talk Radio" and subsequent Oliver Stone film where the talk radio financial host closes his show with something along the lines of "It's not how much you make, it's how much you take HOMMMMMME."

Online and mobile fundraising aren't just a means to the end for "donation access." They are cost effective and can help garner campaign donations in smaller increments, faster and more responsive than traditional fundraising methods.

EXAMPLE: Joe Candidate is running for School Board in a town near you. Joe has friends and family, a list of all of the people from the little league where he's Vice President of Equipment, and a small company with 500 local customers. So let's call the starting list 1,000.

He's got all of their email addresses and has a relationship with them of some sorts. This is a good starting point! He also has 500 professional contacts on Linkedin, 246 "Friends" on Facebook, and 962 Twitter followers.

So, 1,000 + 500 + 246 +962 = 2,708

5% of 2,708 = 135

$10 x 135 = $1,350—that's *Round 1.*

Round 2: Thank the 135 $10 people and ask them to ask their friends, and maybe give another $10 because "we agree." And it's only $10.

Round 3: Follow the news and pick an issue—Example: A $10 Million bond issue is about to happen that includes $10,000 per campus in the district for a statue that proclaims or exhibits something you don't agree with being instituted with taxpayer funds. Ask for $10 to help make sure this nonsense doesn't happen now, again or ever.

Round 4: Thank everyone and ask again this time for $5 or $50.

Leverage your contacts, expand your reach and go for smaller amounts, and track your donors, why they donated, when they donated, how they donated.

Utilizing your database and online "asking" is the best and most cost effective place to start your fundraising. Enabling your database with continued "asks" is a no-brainer, go for small amounts, they add up quickly.

Don't forget about your State, Local and Federal reporting requirements.

17 BLOGS AND NEWS DESTINATIONS

In this age of the 24 hour news cycle on the Internet and mobile devices, the traditional "Letter to the Editor" almost seems like a thing of the past. They are not, but there are a lot more "editors" and a lot more places which are also useful to getting your message out and reaching potential voters or supporters.

If you are a candidate you hope to be a "newsmaker." It's similar if you're an issue-based organization or an individual trying to get your point across. However, most of the time we are "News Chasers" or Advocates utilizing social networks, online news destinations, political commentary sites and issue oriented portals—and of course the web and mobile destinations of our elected officials.

Whether you are a candidate, an advocate or organization, you'll need to start by getting setup and understanding how it works. We'll setup some examples for you at the end.

In nearly all cases, local and national news sites, political sites such as Politico, The Huffington Post, and local political blogs offer a "comment section." Here's where you go to work.

There are basically four types of comment sections with regard to "who you are:"

(1) **Login with your Facebook, Google+ or Twitter account**—this will show your picture and be "clickable" to your Facebook profile. When logging in to either of these accounts, your comment, along with a link and headline for the original story, will most likely also appear in your Facebook conversations/Twitter account.

(2) **Login with Discus**—a third party comment and sharing service—get an account. Its free and widely used.

(3) **Login with your Account & Password**—here you create an account on the specific site you are commenting upon.

(4) **No Login**: Many sites, especially those built on WordPress, Blogger or another platform do not require you to login, but do afford you the opportunity to enter your email address and a website link in order to comment. These are most likely "human edited" sites which review your comment before letting it go live in order to cut down on spam or other garbage that might find its way to their site. ALWAYS put in your email and web address. You might consider setting up an email specifically for commenting. Most of these sites use a Gravatar (a free Avatar service provided by WordPress—your picture and profile follow you around wherever you post information or comment using that email address) to display your image and additional "click through" information. Get one here http://www.gravatar.com.

The object of the exercise is to get your position and name/office in front of the audience that is being generated by the news site and engage potential voters and supporters.

Many voters are "single issue" voters—abortion, gun control, taxes, education, national defense, immigration, etc. Single issue voters are almost always in DISTRESS about their issue and usually complain that "No One Listens to Me." Here's your chance to get in front of them and at least be the one that "Listens."

There are some basic rules and strategies when engaging an online audience this way:

1. Never get into a fight with a skunk!

2. Stay current on the conversation. If someone responds and it's appropriate for you to continue the conversation or answer a question, do it promptly before you lose their attention.

3. Stay consistent. Sometimes it's difficult not to be swayed by a good argument, or at least a well crafted one. Don't shift gears on line, rather take a thoughtful look at your position and see if you might make a change or addition to your policies or leanings. This doesn't mean you are adamant and rigid and not open to new ideas, simply

have your argument and talking points thought out before you make a change.

4. Always say thank you to others when they agree/disagree or comment on anything you wrote.

5. Keep the conversation going both on the "news destination" and hopefully transfer some of those participants to your website and database.

NOTE:This should go without saying, but it is a hazard to be aware of. Don't enjoin conversations when you are worn out, had a couple of drinks, are angry, or in a questionable situation where there is someone with a camera on their mobile phone!

Here's an *Advocate* example:

1. You are an advocate of *Position XYZ* on Healthcare Reform and an article appears on the website of your local paper or television station regarding the discovery of $150 million in fraudulent Medicare billings. Regardless of whether you are for or against national healthcare, everyone agrees that fraudulent billings are not a good thing. You've already setup your logins, and for easier use made sure they are saved in your preferred browser for nearly one-click logins.

   Create your own newsfeeds using HootSuite, or a free RSS reader like Feedly (http://feedly.com) via the web and mobile to stay on top of the "news." Make sure you include the candidates in your area that you support or wish to influence.

   As an Example: my feed would include keywords like *Scottsdale,Arizona,Immigration,Taxes,Education,Crime,Politics,Elections,Diamondbacks,Things to Do,Conlan* (feel free to add stuff like Things to Do while you're at it!) It's a good idea to use your Feed Reader to directly pick up the feeds from a candidate or organization via RSS (Real Simple Syndication).

   Example: subscribe to http://www.politico.com/rss/

2. Follow them and comment on the stories that are appropriate to your cause or candidate.

3. Repost your comments and conversation on Facebook and Twitter, especially if you're really into it and are segmenting Friends and Groups (other people's or the one's that you have created and promoted). It's probably a good idea to NOT Facebook and Twitter if you are cross-posting (meaning everything you put on Facebook shows up on Twitter). Try to avoid duplication.

Here's a *Candidate* Example:

As a Candidate your strategy is divided into two parts—YOUR Strategy and YOUR PEOPLE'S Strategy.

YOUR PEOPLE'S STRATEGY is essentially what you give them "to do" in support of your spreading your message—"like" or share your comment, retweet, post their own comments, encourage friends to follow you or volunteer, etc.

YOUR Strategy: As a Candidate or the point person for an organization the focus on how your strategy develops should be directed toward rapid implementation versus SWOT charts (a method used to evaluate the **S**trengths, **W**eaknesses, **O**pportunities, and **T**hreats involved in a project or business venture and Cost Benefit Analysis). This shouldn't cost anything with a proper implementation plan.

Your implementation plan needs to include:

1. DATA COLLECTION & MANAGEMENT: Figure out the best way(s) for supporters to register and subscribe, define your strategy delivery—email, social media, mobile/text, video, fundraising, all of the above—but segmented.

2. FINDING YOUR FRIENDS: your "friends" are anyone who gives you permission to contact them.

3. FINDING YOUR "REAL FRIENDS": your real friends are the ones that consistently support you on social networks and speak intelligently about your positions, your candidacy, or the efficacy of your organization's solution to a problem. If possible, segment out

your database by type and message. For example: don't send text messages about protest marches to significant contributors, they gave you the contribution in lieu of marching!

4. CRAFTING YOUR MESSAGE: You might want to look at your "message" on two fronts here—the one you put out there under your own name, and the one asking for endorsement. If you have collected data, segmented it and formulated a strategy based upon that data, you might want to try engaging your supporters on a specific issue by providing them the link to your comment and asking them to engage. If you have an Army, you might be able to help them craft "their message" in support of you in advance! Do your best to drive them to Name Identification or engagement on your web, social and mobile media properties.

5. DEPLOYMENT: Find the smartest and most engaging person(s) on your team and put them in charge of this one. Let them sub-contract **movement**, but not position. At the last minute the "change over voter" is potentially going to make your day. And we cast our votes in real time!

It's best that you craft your message, and strategy almost before you begin collecting data. The political environment and data move very quickly.

The best advice is to understand and embrace the concept of **FORCE MULTIPLICATION**, not only for your comments, but the comments of your supporters and the general electorate as well.

18 CAMPAIGN MANAGEMENT SOFTWARE

Depending upon the size, scope and budget of your campaign, using Campaign Management Software is probably a good idea.

Political Campaign Management software can provide financial, marketing and management tools, contribution tracking, voter database and other features to help political candidates, issue advocacy groups and Political Action Committees more effectively manage their campaigns.

Campaign managers use these software applications to efficiently identify likely donors, target voters for outreach efforts, manage volunteers, track contributions and assess the effectiveness of campaigns. Political Campaign software also typically offers demographic and voter behavior data, polling tools, call center integration and other campaign management necessities such as regulatory compliance monitoring.

Examples of campaign software are:

TrailBlazer (http://www.trailblz.com)

Trail Blazer's *Political Campaign Manager* software provides an integrated platform for political campaign management. Campaigns and political action committees (PACs & SuperPACs) can have everything in one place.

Trail Blazer's integrated campaign software targets key voting blocks and tracks voter histories with ease. It tracks every online contribution, fundraising event, volunteer registration, key issue, lawn sign registration and a slew of other fields.

For door-to-door canvassing and access on the go, TrailBlazer offers a convenience of *Mobile Base Camp* from any mobile device. It's bundled for free with the base *Political Campaign Manager* software. Field managers have the flexibility of mobile canvassing tools at their fingertips which saves time and money and the hassle of paper walk lists.

You can coordinate outbound calling with easy-to-read call book reports. You can record every call's content in log notes so everyone knows what's been said to each voter.

TrailBlazer has state-of-the-art communication tools to help you get your message out with built-in mail merge and mass email tools which allow you to track your email opens and links intelligently.

It helps you create successful fundraising events, sell tickets, books, and bumper stickers with an online merchandising feature. You can use shared calendars and reminders to make sure every volunteer knows what task is assigned and what the plan is overall.

You can monitor opinion and voter behavior as well.

The software takes care of FEC Compliance Reporting and required reporting for some states.

You can test drive a free demo at 1-800-446-1375 or contact them at **info@trailblz.com**.

NationBuilder (http://nationbuilder.com). This is their write up:

"NationBuilder is the world's first Community Organizing System: an accessible, affordable, complete software platform that helps leaders grow and organize communities to achieve great things. NationBuilder seamlessly weaves together customizable and easy-to-update websites with a comprehensive contacts database and messaging tools like email newsletters, group text alerts and social media management. Businesses, nonprofits, governments, and politicians use NationBuilder to bring together their online and offline outreach and engagement, allowing them to build more meaningful relationships with customers, supporters, and constituents. NationBuilder was founded by CEO Jim Gilliam and co-founded by President Joe Green and Lead Designer Jesse Haff. The company is based in Los Angeles."

I can vouch for TrailBlazer, Aristotle and NationBuilder as solid tools for success. Don't try and shave a few bucks off of your campaign software solution. There is an affordable solution that will meet your needs.

Aristotle (http://aristotle.com)

Aristotle is an established all in one campaign solution company that has everything you could imagine for political campaign management. International, PACS, Fundraising, Lists, and software and solutions for just about every scenario.

Complete Campaigns (http://completecampaigns.com)

Complete Campaigns was acquired by Aristotle in 2008 is a leader in technology solutions for political campaigns and offers a variety of specific solutions for Federal, State, and local campaigns, PACS and more. They also have a site that is chock full of useful articles.

Here are some others that are available but did not respond to my request for information:

Camelot (http://camelotapp.com)

MyPoliticalManager (http://mypoliticalmanager.com)

AmericanGOTV (http://political-campaign-management-software.com)

19 EMAIL, ROBO CALLS AND MOBILE MARKETING

Obtaining successful email marketing results really isn't that complicated.

Remember THE MESSAGE IS THE MEDIUM and you will be fine.

Before we talk about the message, let's define the differing types of email campaigning you might engage:

BULK: read this one as "well-educated political spam"—except that it gets opened! You get a list from the County or State or Party that includes emails, or maybe an organization that supports you offers to send an email to their members highlighting your avocation of their cause. Or you have the money to purchase a list from a broker, or, even better, call a professional political database engineering firm like CampaignGrid and drill it down to almost anything you can think of that a voter might want! You're trolling for new people, and hopefully mining your loyal followers.

SUBSCRIBERS: anybody that subscribes to your newsletter, registers for any reason, donates, etc. This is your "everybody" class. This is your biggest list and the one you need to ULTIMATELY not abuse. It's probably a better idea to send out HTML "newsletters" or updates that cover your schedule and "opinions" than to send specific requests.

TACTICAL: separate your money people from your volunteers from your followers, from your supporters, from your voters, based upon the data you collect and organize. The "money" people get money emails, the volunteers get "volunteer" emails, and so forth.

RESPONSIVE: every time ANYONE interacts with your digital campaign, on any platform you should have the opportunity to customize your RESPONSE. Take advantage of the space and don't simply go with the defaults.

Default Example: Thanks for Contributing to my campaign. I really appreciate it.

Contact us at: 703-555-1212, info@mycampaign.com, visit www.mycampaign.com Follow Us on Twitter, Like us on Facebook, etc.

Better version: Thanks <insert first name> for recognizing we have a lot of work to do and for contributing your hard earned dollars to my campaign.

I want you to know that you can call me anytime directly at XXX-XXX-XXXX. If I'm on the phone it will roll over to Mary or one of her team. We're doing things a bit differently and deploying a new communication strategy that puts the voter first!

If you haven't had the opportunity to get fully registered on our website www.IMINCHARGEHERE.com please do and let's start the great debate and share it with your friends.

CLICK HERE for an invitation to our next fundraising lunch with important people like you.

CLICK HERE to sign up with Facebook or Twitter

CLICK HERE to talk to Mary about how we can help or if you'd like me to meet with your organization or for a cup of coffee.

Put the Default Contact Information included here with an invitation to the next "event"

Customize each response based upon the action of the potential voter, contributor or supporter. If you are using campaign management software like Trail Blazer or NationBuilder, or even a WordPress Plugin you should be able to configure and modify these responses at will dictated by their "response," based upon your message or schedule.

The goal is to get "thank yous back in spades" from your responsive thank you messages.

THE MESSAGE: Most people get enough garbage in their email. Don't become one of the annoying e-mailers whose messages end up in the trash.

The Golden Rule applies to email, mobile and almost all forms of marketing—don't send something that you wouldn't be interested in at least being alerted to "what's up with the what's up." That's much better than being on the receiving end of this comment "Oh, it's just that politician asking me for money again." Appreciate your audience by delivering actionable items they might enjoy.

There are three key components to successful email messages.

- **SUBJECT LINE**: This is the one that makes a voter want to open it up in the first place. Time and date driven subject lines are a good start. RSVP is a good one too! If your platform or solution affords you the opportunity customize this to read "Bob—BBQ with Candidate X at 111222 E. Showboat Lane This Friday 6PM—Please RSVP.

- **BODY:** Just because at some point you become sick of yourself and the campaign doesn't mean that everyone else is equally worn out! Remind the voter they are excited about being excited about you, and give them something to do!

- **CONTACT SIGNATURE**: Always make sure to give ALL of your contact information, and if available a direct link to the event or action you want the recipient to take action upon.

There are many ways you can effectively deploy email throughout your campaign. Always collect as much data as you can get, and ALWAYS deliver the most voter specific and actionable message possible.

If properly deployed, email (and mobile messaging) can be one of the most effective tools in your campaign strategy.

Worst case scenario, take the best examples from your competitor or colleague!

As with all marketing mediums in the political spectrum, be judicious in its use, otherwise you might be perceived as a pest or wasteful of your contributors donations.

Consider running all of your campaign emails through a service like www.sendgrid.com which offer multiple sending IP addresses to reduce the possibility of your email showing up in spam folders, as well as a unique set of tracking mechanisms that are useful for tweaking your message.

ROBO CALLS

We all know what "RoboCalls" are—the somewhat annoying automated phone call that gives a (hopefully) brief and to the point recorded message from a candidate or policy group urging some action. They are cost effective in terms of your spend, but whether they work or not is up to you to decide! Nothing can replace real people on the phone, except for real people from "the neighborhood" calling their neighbors on your behalf!

There is debate on the effectiveness of RoboCalls, but here are some do's and don'ts to help guide you.

RoboCall Do's

- Put the guts of your message up front before the "answerer" hangs up the phone!

- Differentiate your message from everyone else's message. Don't be afraid to go "Hollywood" with music, special effects, or even an "interview" or "This just in..." announcement.

- Keep it as short as possible

- Be creative—depending upon your RoboCall provider you might be able to take a poll, gauge potential voter turnout, identify supporters, or even solicit donations (be careful with this one, don't hit "unknowns" up for money, especially on your first call. Hopefully you are working off of a "complete" database with at least names and addresses that match up to the list. If so, you might be consider using the RoboCall as an "invite"—"Press 1 to receive an invitation to the Candidate BBQ", "Press 2 to Request an invitation to the next event"—theoretically you could give them an "unsubscribe" option here, but if your local/state regulations don't require it, they'll just hang up if they don't want option 1 or 2!

- Limit and plan the number of calls you put into rotation.

- Obey the law. Your provider should know the laws and be able to supply you with copies and compliance explanations for your locality. Ask them, then as Ronald Reagan made famous "Trust, but Verify"! Many states require the disclosure of who paid for the call, often requiring such notice be recorded in the candidate's own voice, along with a phone number to call to opt-out.

RoboCall Don'ts

- Don't be ANNOYING! RoboCalls can be a two-edged sword. You more than likely will irritate an equal number to the one's you please. Don't call too often. Don't call with the same message twice. Follow the Do's above!

- Don't send a message that you wouldn't want printed in the newspaper or recorded and put on Facebook!

- Don't call people who can't vote, and don't bother calling people outside your party who can't vote in a primary (unless your State allows open primaries).

- Don't bloviate! There are already enough long winded political messages No one wants to listen to it on their phone!

- RoboCalls can be effective. If they weren't, no one would use them! However, they can also be an irritant to potential voters. Be careful!

For more information about RoboCalls, or to find a list of current providers, visit http://www.guidetowinningelections.com.

MOBILE MARKETING

According to the Pew Research Center, as of September 2012 88% of registered voters own a cell phone. Here are some interesting facts about mobile marketing.

Cell Phones and the future of political fundraising and marketing.

- 27% of registered voters who use a cell phone used their phones during the 2012 election cycle to follow campaigns or check political news in general.

- 75% of that group used their cell phone to send and receive text messages.

- 19% sent messages related to a campaign to family, friends or others.

- 5% signed up to receive messages directly from candidates or other groups involved in the campaign.

- 5% say they received unwanted election messages that they didn't sign up to receive.

- Smartphone owners are an even more engaged group. 48% of registered voters own a smartphone.

- 45% of smartphone users have used their smartphone to read other's comments on a social network about a candidate or a campaign in general.

- 35% used their smartphone during the 2012 election cycle to look up information about a candidate to discover whether or not what they just heard was true or not.

- 18% used their smartphone to post their own comments on a social network regarding a candidate or a campaign in general.

- 27% of those watching election night results used both their television and their computer or smartphone.

- **10% of 2012 Presidential donors donated through text or cell-phone apps.**

Source: Pew Research Center's Internet & American Life Project
http://pewInternet.org/Reports/2012/Election-2012-Mobile.aspx

20 INFLUENCING LEGISLATION

The reason you became involved in a political campaign was, mainly, that you believed certain issues should be dealt with in a particular way and you wanted to elect a person to public office who would translate a shared political philosophy into good legislation. In other words, you wanted someone in office who would represent *your* thinking when he voted on legislative matters. So winning the election does not mean it is time for you and the other people who worked in his campaign to relax and forget that politics exists! NEVER! Now is the time to support your newly elected official so that he/she has no qualms about sticking his neck out on controversial issues and vote the way his "constituents" (you) urge him to do. If for some reason your candidate did not win the election, the winner is certainly going to want all the support he can get from *you*, the opposition. (After all, he will be up for re-election all too soon). He will tend to vote in the direction where the strength is—so make YOUR strength known.

In Washington, D.C., in the United States Congress, there are powerful Lobbies. For example, the Labor Unions have employed people who stand at the door to the floor of the House of Representatives when there is a vote on a bill important to Labor. As the Congressmen and Congresswomen enter, he tells the ones who are sympathetic or who "owe" a favor to labor, "The vote on this Bill is YES," or "The vote on this Bill is NO!" He keeps an accurate record of how the votes are cast. The ones who vote "improperly" on several pieces of legislation can be sure they will not receive a campaign contribution, campaign workers, or an endorsement from labor leaders in the next campaign.

This situation really defines lobbying! Lobbying is influencing the outcome of any piece of legislation. It gets its name because those with a special interest in certain legislation began to contact the Senator or Representative in the Lobby of the House or Senate before the Legislator went in to cast his vote. Now lobbying has become a "profession" at every level of government. It's as powerful in state government as it is at the federal level and it operates in almost every organization—the PTA, the city council, and county seats of government. Wherever rules are made, lobbyists exists in some form.

Many large corporations or special interest groups have paid staff working in Governmental Affairs Departments of the company or interest group headquarters. For example, some of the major retailers have lobbyists in Washington as well as in various state governments, companies such as Walmart and Sears. Special interest groups such as the National Education Association, The National Federation of Independent Businesses and the American Medical Association, to name a few, have strong lobbies in Washington. Spend some time in your own state legislature and you will find that they are a powerful influence there as well. In fact some consider them the unofficial lawmakers.

But don't let these highly funded groups and fancy titles scare you. YOU can organize a powerful lobby right there in your own town, county or state—or all three—and at the same time make a powerful impact on your Senators and Representatives in Washington. Just find some like-minded people and get to work—because now we are going to look at "How to Lobby Successfully."

HOW TO LOBBY

Basically, there are two approaches to lobbying your Senator or Congressman: Direct Lobbying or Indirect Lobbying.

Direct lobbying includes:

• Personal visits	• Testifying before committee
• Letters	• Postcard campaigns
• Telephone/text messaging	• Petition Drives
• Telegrams and Mailgrams	• E-mail campaigns

Indirect lobbying includes

- Letters to the editor

- Social media campaigns

- Direct mail to other voters

DIRECT LOBBYING

Personal Visits

When you really want to accomplish some business with another person—when it is critical that you do so—what do you do? Very simple! You go see them! Congressmen and Senators *don't hide* in a box when they are not on the floor of the Senate or House—they have an office. In fact, they have an office in Washington and at least one office in their district which you can visit. When you are concerned with a piece of legislation, go discuss it with him. Do not worry that he will not see you. Remember you are a precinct worker—you have influence over the way your neighbors vote! Perhaps you are presently a precinct captain—in that case, the Congressman or Senator may invite you for coffee or lunch. If you are a District or Area Chairman over several precints, he will invite you for lunch and he definitely will pay!

Visits to His District Office

The district office handles matters that deal directly with his constituents—casework problems such as problems a person has with the Social Security Office or relief from the bureaucracy. It is the responsibility of the district office to keep the official informed about who comes in, what phone calls are coming in, what is in the mail, and what the local papers are saying.

Because the Congressman or Senator is periodically in his district office it is possible to make an appointment for you and others in your group to see him and discuss your concerns about specific legislation.

If the Senator or Congressman is not going to be in the district office talk to his Administrative Assistant—this is his "right hand man" (or woman) and he can relay your thoughts, interests, opinions directly to his boss. The assistant's job is dependent upon accurately representing the Congressman or Senator, which makes him a good person to know. Besides that, you maybe on a "first name basis" with his administrative assistant since both of you were active in the campaign.

Visits to the Washington Office

If you are going to be in Washington, D.C., or are making a special trip to see the Congressman or Senator, it is wise to alert the office staff of your intended visit and schedule an appointment. But remember that he is a very busy person. His schedule includes being present on the floor for voting and debates, attending committee meetings, managing the office, meeting with delegations from his home state, handling constituent problems and going out on speaking engagements. You may have to talk with him as he runs across the lawn or through the halls to get to the House Floor for a Roll Call vote or wait in his office for a bit while he completes some other job. But rest assured, if you are a person who influences votes back home, he *will* make time to see you.

You may find that the person who can help you most in relation to specific legislation is his Legislative Aide. Do not feel slighted if his secretary recommends this in addition to your appointment with the Senator or Congressman. The Legislative Aide knows the current status of all legislation and what your Representative's stand on it may be. He also knows where pressure needs to be exerted to help pass or block certain pieces of legislation. You should make the Legislative Aide one of your best political friends.

If you have time to do some sightseeing while you are in Washington, your Senator or Congressman can make your stay more exciting and informative. If you let him or her know well in advance of your visit, his staff can arrange a tour of the White House, get tickets for sessions in the House and Senate, arrange for you to attend committee meetings that may be of interest to you, get special tours of the Federal Bureau of Investigation and other places of interest in Washington.

Letters

A "rule of thumb" in the United States Congress is: *Every one letter that a Congressman or Senator receives from a constituent about a certain piece of legislation usually represents about 100 others that would have written representing that point of view, if those constituents had gotten around to writing.* Therefore, 50 letters in favor of or against a bill represents the thinking of 5,000 constituents—a number not to be sneezed at (Remember, 250 people working together can put almost anyone in or out of Congress or only 50-100 dedicated precinct workers can defeat almost any state representative or city councilman who is not responsive to their thinking. (There is not, at this time a rule of thumb for e-mail. It still is influential but because of its ease to mail and forward, it is not as powerful as a written, stamped and mailed letter).

Writing a good letter takes time and effort, but can make a powerful impact. Generally you can use the following format when writing to your Representative, but this is not an iron clad rule:

First Paragraph:

A very short introduction of yourself and a word of praise or commendation (even public officials like to hear something positive now and then and, surely, you can find something good to comment on even for the representative whose voting record is the problem).

Second Paragraph:

Specify the issue or Bill about which you are concerned.

Third Paragraph:

Tell him why you are concerned, including costs, philosophical objections, academic arguments, emotional concerns—any reasons you think will make your argument valid and effective.

Fourth Paragraph:

Let him know you look forward to his reply so you can share it with "all your friends" at the club, at church, at the lodge, at the "district meetings" etc. Ask him specific questions so his reply cannot be a form letter. If you are urging him to vote a certain way, ask him to inform you of how he plans to vote, what the outcome of the voting was, and, if the bill passed, did the bill pass with or without amendments. If amended, what were the key changes and how did he vote on it.

OTHER SUGGESTIONS

- Use business, school, or association stationery if you have it, or identify yourself as a precinct committeeman or captain. That increases your credibility as a representative of more than one voter. Sign your name over your typed signature at the end

- Be sure your exact address is on the letter.

- Keep to the point. Discuss one issue only, stating the name of the bill you are writing about and the bill number if you know it.

- You are not trying to "convert" the member to your philosophy or religion. Your aim is to urge him to vote *your way* on certain legislation.

- Be sure you know your facts. Never make charges you cannot support. Do not *ever* depend on what someone else has told you. If you can, enclose newspaper articles, editorials or fact sheets to back up your arguments.

- Make your letter personal. Stress how the legislation will affect you, your job, family business and/or community. Never use a form letter—they only reveal that you are unable to express your own views.

- Be reasonable, not asking for the impossible.

- Do not threaten. EVER!

- Be constructive. If you think the bill is the wrong approach to a problem say so, but offer some positive suggestions about a better approach, if there is one.

- Concentrate only on the Senators and Representatives from your own state. You cannot vote for any of the others—or against them—so their correspondence secretary probably will ignore you or send your letter to your own Representative...or the waste basket.

- Be sure to identify yourself as a voter, a person who worked in his campaign, as a fund raiser, a civic organization leader, as a precinct committeeman—whatever tie you may happen to have.

- If you have contributed to his campaign, correspond often, or know him personally, it is certainly acceptable to use his first name and sign your first name only (as long as your last name is typed below it).

- You may not need to correspond to the member directly; rather, you may want to write his legislative assistant directly.

- When he votes *your way*, write to thank him. He will both appreciate it and remember it. Everyone needs a pat on the back now and then. If however, he did not vote "your way," let him know of your disappointment.

- If he does not answer your questions, write him again. A clever way for politicians to reply is "Thank you for your views on _____. You can be assured I will keep them in mind when the bill comes before the full Senate." If he does not say specifically how he intends to vote, it is either because he truly does not know how he intends to vote, or more likely he is fence-sitting, trying to avoid the heat. You and your friends need to bombard him with letters and calls to get him "off the fence."

ADDRESSES AND SALUTATIONS FOR INDIVIDUALS AND ORGANIZATIONS

Government Official	*Salutation*
President _____ The White House Washington, D.C. 20500	Dear Mr./Ms. _____
The Honorable _____ The United States Senate Washington, D.C. 20510	Dear Senator_____
The Honorable _____ The House of Representatives Washington, D.C. 20515	Dear Congressman _____ or Dear Congresswoman _____
Justice_____ Supreme Court Washington, D.C. 20543	Dear Justice _____
The Honorable_____ Department of State Washington, D.C. 20520	Dear Mr./Ms. _____
The Honorable _____ Department of Education 400 Maryland Ave, SW Washington, DC 20202	Dear Mr./Ms. _____
The Honorable _____ Department of Labor 200 Constitution Ave., NW Washington, DC 20210	Dear Mr./Ms. _____

For a full listing go to http://www.guidetowinningelections.com

LOBBYING BY TELEPHONE AND/OR E-MAIL

Telephone

There are times when there is simply not enough time to do your lobbying by letter; therefore, the best way to handle it is by phone or email. "But," you say, "One person can't make much of an impact." Correct! This is where a telephone network comes into play.

One person can make ten calls (or text) to different people in about thirty minutes. And those ten people could make ten calls to ten additional people. Each of those one hundred people could make ten calls in their own state and each of those one thousand people could make ten calls to people in their town, organization or social group. And now with Internet phone ability like Skype it is possible to call a group of people at the same time. You can even use video calls if you wish.

In less than two *hours ten thousand people* could be alerted to action—to call their legislator. Can you imagine the thoughts that run through the minds of the legislators and the vision of what will happen in the next election when he starts receiving one thousand phone calls over the next day or two? And remember, every legislator will receive the same overwhelming number of calls if everyone does his/her job.

To do this on national issues you need to develop a source of information you have confidence in and keep current on legislation relevant to your concerns. And you need to make contact with the "point man" in your state who can set your own state operation into action.

The telephone operation is quite simple. At various functions (clubs, lodges, political groups, etc.) you need to recruit people of "like mind" on the issues who are willing to be involved. You need to find a "point" man or woman in every city who can organize and activate their telephone committee. When you set it into action it will go something like this: One person at the state level who has all the facts about the legislation or issue calls or texts ten key people around the state. They in turn call or text ten people in various towns. Each of these contacts ten and each of these contacts ten. In a matter of hours people all around the state are calling their state senators and representatives. You can do this on a county or city level as well. All you need is the point person and names and numbers of who to call.

E-mail

An e-mail chain works the same way only you can reach larger numbers of people in much less time. Make a contact list for political contacts. You can initiate it or respond to someone else's initiation. To make it most effective:

Do not simply hit "forward" and send it out with all the "old" information on it. Cut and past the message into a new e-mail window and send it to your list.

Ask each receiver to do the same.

On the e-mail you send to the elected official, write the message in your own words instead of doing a copy and paste so he receives an original message. Ask each member on your list to do the same.

An easy way to have volunteers sign up for either the phone or e-mail chain is to have them compete a "phone chain volunteer form" such as the one below. Then you arrange them according to area and assign ten names to each phone volunteer. The important thing is to use it frequently enough to keep your volunteers excited and motivated.

The number of e-mail addresses one person can handle is limitless.

Phone Chain Volunteer

I will call/text people ☐ in my ☐ in my state

I will email ☐ in my area ☐ state ☐ nationwide

Name _____

Address _____

_____

Phone _____

email _____

If phoning, it is extremely important that each caller gets the information exactly correct. Remember the old game of "Gossip?" As a message was passed by whisper from one person to the next it was changed a little bit, and grew more and more distorted as it went from one person to the next. Many times the final message had no resemblance to the message that was given by the originator. You don't want to play "gossip" with your telephone pyramid.

Texting and emailing rather than calling, can eliminate the game of gossip and the garbling of the message. If it needs to be done "voice to voice" email or text the exact message you want the callers to use.

TESTYFYING BEFORE COMMITTEE

Every bill, when it is introduced, is referred to one or more committees or subcommittees. This is the best place to influence legislation. These committees, made up of legislators from both political parties, have the task of studying the proposed legislation and reporting their assessment (favorable or unfavorable) to their House or Senate. In the committee you can concentrate your lobbying efforts on a dozen or so legislators and their staffs. If requested by the chairman of the committee or subcommittee, the committee will conduct public hearings on the proposed legislation. At the hearings, the committee members want to hear from those who will be affected by the bill.

The suggestions presented here deal mainly with state legislators and Congressional committees; they would, however, with a little adjustment, apply to city councils and school boards.

HOW TO BE INVITED TO PRESENT TESTIMONY

- **First**: Find out which subcommittee is studying the legislation and who the subcommittee chairman and minority leader are.

- **Second:** Write a letter concerning your interest to the subcommittee chairman and the minority leader asking for an opportunity to appear and submit a written statement and brief oral testimony.

- **Third**: Cover all bases by asking your own local legislator for assistance in getting the invitation

PREPARING YOUR TESTIMONY

1. Know the issue.

    a. Study all testimony already given before the subcommittee.

    b Know what the legislation does—whether it amends, ratifies, or creates new public policy.

2. Keep it brief.

    a. Your oral testimony should be long enough to cover all of your interests, but try to keep it limited to between seven and ten minutes.

    b. Have a summary of your testimony prepared so you will not have to read your full testimony in its entirety.

3. Make approximately 50 copies of your statement and oral testimony. These are usually given to the Congressional subcommittees 48 hours before you testify. At the city council or state legislature level fewer copies are needed.

    a) The name of your organization should be in the heading. Use organization stationery if possible.

    b) The name of the president of your organization and your name should be in capital letters.

    c) The salutation should be addressed to Mr. or Madam Chairman.

3. Include in your testimony:

    d) Facts, not emotion. Know what you are talking about.

    e) The identity of your organization.

    f) Your basic interest concerning the legislation.

    g) What you want added to, deleted from or changed in the bill...

h) Be prepared to answer any questions the committee members may have.

After you have presented your testimony, it will be studied by the staff—seldom in detail by the elected official. That is why your brief oral presentation is so important. Your testimony could make the difference between good and bad legislation; therefore, it is critical that you do your homework and come prepared.

LOBBYING WITH POSTCARDS

Postcards are an inexpensive way to influence legislation and public policy. Keep it simple. Have a few sentences on the back expressing your opposition to or support for a bill or issue. The key to success in a postcard effort is to have thousands of postcards delivered to the Senator or Congressman you are trying to influence.

Your group could get postcards printed or buy assorted picture postcards. Preferably, each person should write his/her own message. Each card should be signed with name and address. At your next meeting, you can hand out the postcard, have them signed if the message is already printed, or have the message written by each member. Do this at each meeting of any group you attend. Ask them to turn them in to you with the cost of postage (at this writing postage for a regular sized postcard is $0.33 and an oversized postcard is $0.46) You can then be sure that all of them get into the mail as soon as possible.

PETITIONS

Petitions can be used to show broad support for an issue or cause, to get an issue on the ballot for an "initiative" vote by all the people (in some states only), and to show dissatisfaction with a current situation or condition, or unsatisfactory pieces of legislation.

When writing a petition:

- Keep the statement of purpose to one short paragraph

- Specify clearly who is being petitioned—the Congress, the City Council, the School Board, etc.

- Leave plenty of room for the signers

- Include columns for name, address, city/state/zip/phone

- Provide a space for the person who circulates the petition to put his name, address and phone number.

- Be sure to have on each petition the address to which it should be mailed or delivered when it is completed. Have only ONE collection point.

- Have a clear deadline for the return of all petitions. If your petition is for a candidate, initiative, recall or other legal purpose, be sure to check with the Secretary of State of your state for guidelines *before* printing the petition or beginning the signature collection drive.

- Be sure to make a copy of each petition before sending it to the person or organization you are petitioning. This list of names can be quite valuable to you in other political endeavors.

Generally, petitions are the weakest tool to use in lobbying. There is the possibility that many of the signatures are not valid; there is also the possibility that people sign a petition without understanding the issue or bill it is supporting or opposing. Legislators give far less weight to petitions than they do to personal letters or telephone calls.

INDIRECT LOBBYING

Letters to the Editor

The editorial page of your local paper offers a superb forum for lobbying and gaining support for your position. This may be for print or on-line editions. Writing letters to the editor takes thoughtfulness. If they are to be printed and make an impact, they must be done correctly and skillfully.

You will probably find instructions and guidelines for writing letters to the editor on the editorial page of your local paper. For example, the instructions will most likely tell you to sign the letter and include an address and phone number where you can be reached during the day.

All letters on behalf of a candidate or issue will not be published. However, if you write or email frequently, your chances of being published increase. Some things you may want to write about include your agreement or disagreement with an editorial the paper published; your reaction to a newsworthy event; your approval or disapproval of the way the paper is presenting the news on a subject—whether it is fair or biased, accurate or sloppy; your comments on a community, state or national problem (pornography, alcoholism, drug abuse, education, foreign affairs); your suggested solution to that problem; and your assessment of the performance of elected officials.

In writing letters to the editor you should keep in mind the following suggestions:

- Remember your audience. It is not so much the editor—it is the thousands of readers whose thinking you want to sway.
- Keep it brief.
- Avoid name calling.
- Always be courteous and gently persuasive for the newspaper reader
- Define the problem and offer a solution or recommendation.

Using Digital Media

An effective means of voicing your opinion is using digital media: blogs, Twitter, Social Networking sites like Facebook, Myspace and Linkedin, YouTube and Press Releases. See Chapter 15 on Social Media

Now you know what the pros know about lobbying. YOU can do the same high quality job they do if you think clearly, organize and communicate politely. With you and others of like mind joining together, the elected representatives on your local, state and national level will finally hear the voice of the voters again.

ABOUT THE AUTHOR

C. Douglas Conlan is a 20 year marketing veteran having served United States Senators, Congressmen and local School Board Members in their campaigns with local staffing, constituent services, fundraising and media relations. His legislative action background includes helping draft cost reduction and pro-environment legislation bringing Republicans and Democrats together. Mr. Conlan helped found VoiceAmerica.com, today one of the largest and most profitable closely held Internet Broadcasting enterprises. He studied Marketing at the University of Tampa and Political Science at George Mason University.

To Order Additional or Bulk copies please visit:

www.guidetowinningelections.com

www.ingramcontent.com/pod-product-compliance
Lightning Source LLC
Chambersburg PA
CBHW070650290526
45790CB00001B/256